DAYTON

DAYTON

The Rise, Decline, and Transition
of an Industrial City

ADAM A. MILLSAP

TRILLIUM, AN IMPRINT OF
THE OHIO STATE UNIVERSITY PRESS
COLUMBUS

Library of Congress Cataloging-in-Publication Data
Names: Millsap, Adam A., author.
Title: Dayton : the rise, decline, and transition of an industrial city / Adam A.
    Millsap.
Other titles: Rise, decline, and transition of an industrial city
Description: Columbus : Trillium, an imprint of the Ohio State University Press,
    [2019] | Includes bibliographical references and index. | Summary: "Examines
    underlying factors behind the rise and decline of Dayton, Ohio, an archetypal
    Rust-Belt city, ultimately proposing a plan for revival."—Provided by
    publisher.
Identifiers: LCCN 2019034278 | ISBN 9780814255551 (paperback) | ISBN
    9780814277379 (ebook) | ISBN 9780814277362 (ebook)
Subjects: LCSH: Dayton (Ohio)—History. | Dayton (Ohio)—Economic conditions. |
    Industries—Ohio—Dayton—History.
Classification: LCC F499.D257 M55 2019 | DDC 977.1/73—dc23
LC record available at https://lccn.loc.gov/2019034278

Cover design by Laurence J. Nozik
Text design by Juliet Williams
Type set in Adobe Palatino

To my family, especially those who settled in Ohio.

CONTENTS

ILLUSTRATIONS

PHOTOS

INTRODUCTION

And our city, shall we fail her?
Or desert her gracious cause?
Nay—with loyalty we hail her
And revere her righteous laws.
She shall ever claim our duty,
For she shines—the brightest gem
That has ever decked with beauty
Dear Ohio's diadem.

—"A TOAST TO DAYTON" (1917) BY
DAYTON NATIVE PAUL LAURENCE DUNBAR

ABANDONED FACTORIES and homes, underused roads, empty lots, and crumbling infrastructure can be found in nearly every city in the Rust Belt—an area that stretches from Missouri to Wisconsin and east to New York. While many of these problems are common to all cities, their pervasiveness in Rust-Belt cities is the inspiration for the epithet. The US population has been shifting rapidly from the Midwest and Northeast to the area referred to as the Sunbelt—which stretches from the Carolinas to Southern California—for the last 70 years, and this population shift has helped hollow out many northern cities. Researchers who have analyzed this shift have found evidence that a preference for milder winters and more sun, cheaper housing, and market-friendly economic policies are some of the biggest contributing factors.

The Rust Belt region has been heavily analyzed by scholars from a variety of disciplines but fewer works focus on a single Rust-Belt city and try to place it in the broader context of regional economic decline. There are thousands of cities within the states that encompass the Rust Belt and each of them, despite sharing many similarities with their neighbors, has its own history. The details of these histories can help us better understand other cities and the region as a whole.

This book focuses on the city of Dayton, Ohio, and explains some of the largest factors that contributed to its decline over the course of the twentieth

1

century.[1] The world is complex, so we shouldn't expect a city's decline to be caused by a single identifiable factor. Instead, a city's growth or decline is a multifaceted process that takes place over many decades and is caused by both outside forces and internal public policies.

On the surface Dayton appears to be a typical midwestern Rust-Belt city, but an analysis of its past reveals its exceptionalism. Though today it's not as prominent as some of its larger Rust-Belt brethren such as Cleveland or Detroit, in the early twentieth century it was a well-known hub of innovation. In 1900 its residents generated more patents per capita than any other large US city, and a few years later Dayton natives Orville and Wilbur Wright—inventors of the first practical flying machine—became two of the most popular people in the world, making their hometown famous.

Yet despite Dayton's early success, its history provides the quintessential example of a Rust-Belt city's life cycle: rapid population growth as the country transitioned from an agricultural economy to an industrial one; relative decline as people left cities for the suburbs; and finally absolute decline as people and jobs left the region altogether for the warmer climates, cheaper housing, and freer economies of the Sunbelt. Today a period of stagnation has set in that has left city officials and residents searching for ways to reclaim previous prosperity.

Before going any further, it's important to define some terms that show up in this book. Metropolitan statistical areas (MSA), or metro areas, are defined by the US Office of Management and Budget and consist of a group of counties that together form a common labor market. Economists often study MSAs rather than political cities since the economic forces that govern the formation and growth of dense clusters of people—that is, cities—typically work across political boundaries. This book, however, focuses on the city of Dayton, or what economists typically denote the "political city" or "central city," and when the word *city* is used in this book it means the political or central city.

There are several reasons why I focus on the city of Dayton rather than the broader metro area. First, city decline is more shocking and interesting. The population declines of big cities like Detroit, Cleveland, and Buffalo are well known and economists and other researchers have spent decades trying to explain them. In this book I apply their findings to the city of Dayton.

The second reason is that the city or municipal government is the most local level of government in the United States. In addition to helping people

---

1. This book builds on the work I began in a paper for the Mercatus Center at George Mason University: Adam A. Millsap, "How the Gem City Lost Its Luster and How It Can Get It Back: A Case Study of Dayton, Ohio," Mercatus Research, Mercatus Center at George Mason University, Arlington, VA, 2017.

understand why cities like Dayton declined, I also offer some recommendations for how cities like Dayton can bounce back. There are no metropolitan
area governments in Ohio, but the state does have a robust home-rule law
that gives a lot of authority to city officials. Thus, many of the policies that
can help Dayton are going to be implemented at the city level, and that is
where I focus.

Finally, the most successful metro areas have successful central cities.
Because of their larger populations and economies, central cities have a significant influence on the smaller surrounding cities that make up the metro
area. It's hard to picture the broader Dayton metro area thriving without a
healthy city of Dayton.

Even though the focus of this book is the city of Dayton, I reference data
from both metro areas and cities, depending on what is being discussed.
Throughout the book I explicitly identify which unit I am referring to in
order to alleviate confusion. *City* refers to what most people think of when
they think of a city. When data from MSAs are being discussed, I use the
term *metro area*.

National Population Shifts

The low population growth in the Midwest and Northeast regions of America over the last several decades is evident at the metro level and county
level. Ohio is located in the East North Central (ENC) division of the country, and the counties in this division had the third-smallest population
growth from 1970 to 2013. County-level growth was only 29%, just ahead
of the Mid-Atlantic division's 23% growth (New York, Pennsylvania, and
New Jersey) but well below the 123% growth in the Mountain division (Arizona, New Mexico, and the states north of them to Montana) and the 110%
growth in the South Atlantic division (Florida and the coastal states north
to Maryland).

An examination of metro area growth from two more recent time periods also reveals that the ENC division fared poorly.[2] From 1990 to 2010 the
large metro areas in the ENC grew slightly faster than the metro areas in
New England (Connecticut and the states north to Maine) and Mid-Atlantic
divisions—13% versus 9% and 10%, respectively. But in the most recent
period, growth slowed down: From 2000 to 2010 the large metro areas in

---

2. The 1990–2010 and 2000–2010 growth amounts were calculated using the 184
MSAs that had more than 250,000 people in 2010.

the ENC only grew by 4.1%, which was the smallest growth of all nine divisions and well short of the Mountain division's 25% growth and the roughly 18% growth in the South Atlantic and West South Central (Texas, Oklahoma, Arkansas, and Louisiana) divisions. Faster growth in the Sunbelt regions means that the percentage of the country's population living in the midwestern and northeastern regions declined over time. People are a valuable resource, so slower population growth reduces prosperity in the Midwest and Northeast relative to the Sunbelt.

This population shift shows little sign of abating. An important driver of this trend is peoples' desire to live in warmer, sunnier climates. Research shows that the demand for sunny, temperate weather increases with income, which means that as per capita incomes rise migration to the Sunbelt is likely to continue.[3]

But while climate and geography are important factors when it comes to the distribution of people across space, they are not the only things that matter. Policies that cultivate economic growth and allow markets to operate are also important, and it is along this dimension that cold weather cities can differentiate themselves. Dayton cannot compete with cities in Florida, Arizona, Southern California, or other large cities along the coasts when it comes to climate or other place-specific amenities like access to beaches. In order to attract people and firms, Dayton officials and voters must compensate for their relatively poor climate and geographic amenities by offering potential migrants a better business and fiscal environment.

In order to understand Dayton's situation today, it helps to know about its past. This book analyzes Dayton and the surrounding region from the turn of the twentieth century to the present. In doing so, the roughly 120 years is divided into three periods based on Dayton's population growth: the turn of the twentieth century to 1930; 1930 to 1960; and 1960 to the early 2000s. The first chapter explains how and why cities like Dayton form. The next four chapters discuss the three periods of Dayton's history. The sixth chapter focuses on Dayton's economic situation today and discusses policies and ideas that can help Dayton prosper going forward. The final chapter offers some concluding remarks.

Figure 1 shows the population of the city of Dayton and Montgomery County, of which Dayton is the county seat, and visualizes the three periods of Dayton's history in terms of population. Dayton was incorporated

---

3. Jordan Rappaport, "Moving to Nice Weather," *Regional Science and Urban Economics* 37, no. 3 (2007): 375–98.

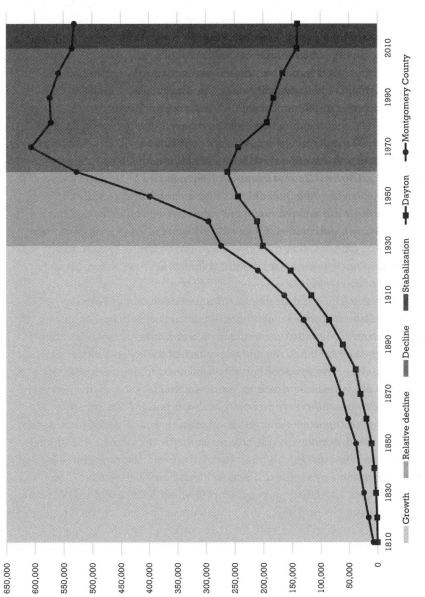

FIGURE 1. Population of Dayton and Montgomery County, 1810–2016. (Data from US Census Bureau.)

Growth   Relative decline   Decline   Stabilization   Dayton   Montgomery County

as a city in 1805 so the data in figure 1 start in 1810, which is the closest census year after incorporation. From 1810 until 1930 it experienced substantial population growth, particularly from 1900 to 1930. Throughout this period, it was the focal point of its region: Its share of the county population increased from 5% in 1810 to 73% in 1930. From 1930 to 1960 Dayton's population continued to increase but at a slower rate, especially when compared to the rest of Montgomery County. During this period, Dayton's share of the county population declined by 23 percentage points, from 73% to 50%. So even though Dayton's population increased from 1930 to 1960, this was a period of relative decline for the city. Migration to the suburban areas began during this period, and nearby communities such as Fairborn, Kettering, and Vandalia grew rapidly.

The next period, from 1960 until 2010, was one of absolute decline for both Dayton and Montgomery County, though the county's decline lagged Dayton's by a decade and was less dramatic. During this period, northern manufacturing declined rapidly and people began migrating to the South and West in larger numbers. Dayton lost nearly half of its population and was one of many midwestern manufacturing cities to experience a large net outflow of residents.

Finally, the most recent period from 2010 onward has been one of relative stability. Dayton's population has hovered around 140,000 during the current decade, but non-decennial-census estimates are imprecise. It remains to be seen whether Dayton's population is still declining, has stabilized, or has started to grow again, but recent estimates hint at further decline.

This book is not a complete history of Dayton, and many details are left out. It does, however, provide enough historical detail for the reader to appreciate the magnitude of Dayton's growth and decline, while also providing context for the underlying causes of its decline. Additionally, the causes analyzed in this book apply to similar municipalities located throughout the Rust Belt, and I hope that readers not from the Dayton area will use the information and analysis presented here to better understand their own cities.

CHAPTER 1

Why Do Big Cities Exist?

A **MERICA IS** a big place: It contains over 3.5 million square miles of land. Yet if you have ever taken a long drive, you've probably noticed that a lot of the land is undeveloped. Instead of being spread out uniformly over the available land, people tend to cluster together. The clustering of people and economic activity is a product of powerful economic forces, and the result of these forces is what we call cities. Before we examine Dayton's story, we need to discuss why big cities exist in the first place. Understanding why cities exist and what benefits they provide will help us better understand why some cities grow and others shrink over time.

The key attribute of a city is the elimination of physical space. At its most basic level, a city is simply a group of people living and working in proximity to one another. This clustering occurs because it's beneficial, and one of the big benefits of clustering is that it reduces transportation costs. When people and firms are located close together, goods have less distance to travel, which makes it cheaper to move them. Cities make it easier for suppliers to get their products to producers, for producers to get their goods to retailers, and for retailers to get the final goods to consumers. Transportation costs can be a large portion of a business's total costs, and when this is the case those businesses have a strong incentive to locate in a city near their suppliers or their customers.

In addition to lower transportation costs, the clustering of people and firms in cities occurs for two reasons: economies of scale and agglomeration economies. A firm has economies of scale when the average cost of producing a good declines as more is produced. A primary reason for declining costs is specialization. When individual workers focus on specific tasks, their individual productivity—and thus the collective productivity of the firm—increases.

For example, one summer while I was in college I worked at a General Motors (GM) manufacturing facility in Moraine, Ohio, located just south of Dayton. Our production goal was around 500 sport utility vehicles (SUVs) per nine-hour shift, and to be that productive we had to work quickly with few mistakes. As Adam Smith discusses in *The Wealth of Nations,* an effective way to do this is to set up production so that each person specializes in a particular task.[1] At the GM facility, my particular task was to install gas tanks on each SUV's frame as it passed by. Even though I had never installed a gas tank and knew almost nothing about how to assemble a car, I became an expert at this one task in less than an hour.

The fact that I didn't know how to do anything else when it came to assembling a car didn't matter because I was surrounded by hundreds of other people who were experts at their individual task. With each of us focusing on one job, mistakes were reduced and the car could move quickly down the assembly line. Collectively, we produced approximately 500 fully assembled SUVs per shift, even though individually none of us could assemble even one car per day.

Specialization reduces mistakes and leads to more output for a given amount of overhead, both of which decrease the average cost of producing a product. An entrepreneur's quest to lower costs to increase profit encourages the formation of large firms that hire dozens of workers who each specialize in only a few tasks. These workers tend to live in proximity to one another, and this clustering of people is the beginning of a city.

In general, the degree of specialization is limited by the size of the market. Since everyone routinely visits a grocery store, it doesn't take a large amount of people to support one. But fewer people in America purchase European sports cars or Ethiopian food, and those who make these purchases do so infrequently. Only bigger cities can support highly specialized employment, dining, and retail options due to their larger number of workers and customers, each with different talents and tastes. Cities are filled with diversity—diverse people, foods, employers, and entertainment

---

1. Adam Smith. *An Inquiry Into the Nature and Causes of the Wealth of Nations.* (London: T. Nelson and Sons, 1887), 3.

options—and this diversity draws in people who value variety and leads to additional population growth.

Of course, greater specialization, and the variety of opportunities it creates, increases the demand for land in cities, which drives up the price of land. The higher price of land in cities limits how populated they can get due to the benefits of specialization alone. In order to explain cities with several hundred thousand, or even millions, of people, there must be another reason people and firms want to cluster together. This brings us to the next big factor that drives city growth—agglomeration economies. Agglomeration economies can be divided into two groups: those that lower the cost of inputs used in the production process and those that make the inputs themselves more productive.[2]

An example of the former is more efficient job matching. Firms that require a very specialized type of worker can often find one more quickly in a big city with a lot of people than in a small town. Similarly, a highly specialized worker, such as a physicist with a PhD, will have an easier time finding a firm that can use her skills in a big city than in a small town. Thus, specialized workers and the firms that need them face lower search costs when they locate in big cities, which leads to large cities becoming even larger as both workers and firms locate there.

The proximity of people in cities also speeds up the transmission of ideas, which is an example of the second type of agglomeration economy. When people get together they talk, and talking transmits information. Regarding how the transmission of ideas contributes to industries clustering in certain places, Economist Alfred Marshall wrote in 1890 that "so great are the advantages which people following the same skilled trade get from near neighborhood to one another. The mysteries of the trade become no mysteries; but are as it were in the air, and children learn many of them unconsciously."[3]

The unintentional and intentional sharing of information and ideas among people in cities—what economists call *knowledge spillovers*—makes workers more productive. This greater productivity has two effects: It increases wages and the opportunity cost of time. Businesses that rely on information, such as those in finance, education, technology, media, and health care, are incentivized to locate in cities in order to take advantage of the rapid exchange of information and the greater productivity of workers. And as wages go up, the opportunity cost of our time increases, which

2. Jan K. Brueckner, *Lectures on Urban Economics* (Cambridge, MA: MIT Press, 2011), 5.

3. Alfred Marshall, *Principles of Economics: An Introductory Volume* (London: Macmillan, 1961), 225.

makes sitting in traffic more expensive and encourages city living. People who have a strong demand for services like restaurant meals, massages, and manicures are especially attracted to cities since those and similar services require face-to-face contact and thus travel. Since cities reduce the physical distance between people, they excel as places for delivering services.

Knowledge spillovers can occur between workers at different firms in the same industry, such as the engineers at Ford and GM sharing ideas over drinks in Detroit or, in a less collegial example, copying ideas from one another. When Dayton inventors and entrepreneurs Charles Kettering and Edward Deeds were experimenting with eight-cylinder engines in 1914, they felt "it was necessary to carry on the experiments in secrecy since Detroit is a rumor factory."[4] Knowledge spillovers can also occur between workers in different industries. These within-industry and across-industry knowledge spillovers are examples of positive externalities, which are benefits that accrue to a person or firm even though that person or firm wasn't involved with the initial activity that created the benefit.

An automotive example is Volvo's creation and subsequent sharing of the design for the three-point seat belt. After introducing the three-point seat belt in 1959 as a replacement for the less effective lap belt, Volvo waived its patent rights to allow other car manufacturers to use its design. This was a positive externality to the other car manufacturers since it allowed them to improve the safety of their vehicles without bearing any of the research and design costs or compensating Volvo.

If within-industry knowledge spillovers are important for economic growth, then cities with a high concentration of employment in one industry will grow faster than similar cities with less concentrated employment. This also implies that a city's success is at least partially tied to the success of its key industries. That is, the film industry in Los Angeles, the automobile industry in Detroit, the technology industry in San Francisco, and the finance industry in New York help drive their respective cities' growth via within-industry knowledge spillovers.

Alternatively, the existence of across-industry spillovers implies that industry variety, not concentration, is important for a city's economic success. It also means that bigger cities that contain more industries and people should be more productive than smaller cities that contain fewer. There is evidence that both types of spillovers are important for city growth, and we will discuss them more throughout the book.

---

4. Isaac Frederick Marcosson, *Colonel Deeds: Industrial Builder* (New York: Dodd, Mead, 1947), 133.

In general, the greater productivity generated by knowledge spillovers—which means higher wages for workers and more revenue for firms—induces workers and firms to locate near one another despite higher land prices. There is also evidence that agglomeration economies have the biggest effect on productivity when they are close to where the production occurs. Economists Stuart Rosenthal and William Strange find that workers and firms benefit most from agglomeration economies that occur within roughly a five-mile radius of their location.[5] The fact that the benefits of clustering decrease with distance encourages economic activity to compress even further. Together, economies of scale and agglomeration economies generate clusters of people and economic activity, and these clusters are our cities.

The types of activity each city specializes in also depends on geography and natural resources. Cities in Hawaii and Florida often have large tourism industries due to the weather and abundant coastline of those states. Cities in the Midwest, such as Dayton, specialized in the production of automobiles, rubber, steel, and coal due to the region's endowment of the necessary resources and the ingenuity of the city's entrepreneurs who discovered valuable ways to use them. The cooler climates of the northern states were also more conducive to manufacturing early on, since prior to the advent of air conditioning factories were largely cooled by the air around them.

Firms clustering in certain cities is possible within the United States because the residents of the 50 states are free to trade with one another. This means it's not necessary for each state to produce everything its residents want to consume. Instead, people and firms in different states can specialize in the production of certain goods and services and then trade for the other things they want. Without the ability to trade, movie studios, financial firms, and car manufacturers would have to be in every state across America or else people would have to go without. The restrictions on barriers to interstate commerce enshrined in the US Constitution created a geographically large and diverse free-trade zone that enabled the industrial clustering that we see today, and we are much wealthier because of it.

Advances in communication technology have routinely generated predictions about the demise of cities. Cities thrive because they eliminate the physical distance between people and facilitate the flow of information. The ability to communicate in real time via telegraph, then telephone, and finally video via technologies like FaceTime and Skype has caused many to question the continued economic importance of actual face-to-face contact. If

5. Stuart S. Rosenthal and William C. Strange, "Geography, Industrial Organization, and Agglomeration," *Review of Economics and Statistics* 85, no. 2 (2003): 377–93; Rosenthal and Strange, "The Attenuation of Human Capital Spillovers," *Journal of Urban Economics* 64 no. 2 (September 2008): 373–89.

technology can deliver the same results without requiring people to crowd together, perhaps we don't need today's dense, concrete jungles.

But instead of declining, cities seem to be just as important as ever. According to the US Census Bureau, in 2015 63% of the people in America lived in cities comprising just 3.5% of the country's land area.[6] When cities are broadened to metropolitan areas, they contain 84% of the country's population. The death of cities in general has been oversold, as they are still important centers of economic growth.

While cities in general are still important, that doesn't mean each individual city is. Dayton and many other cities have been declining for several decades to the detriment of the people who remain in them. A city that is consistently losing population over a long period of time faces a variety of problems, such as increased crime, declining housing values, a decline in the quality of public services, and higher costs in the provision of public services. There is also a psychological cost to residents and city officials: associating population loss with failure. The Tiebout theory of population sorting, named after economist Charles Tiebout, argues that mobile persons who want to maximize their happiness do so by choosing to reside in the location that best matches their preferences for public goods and services.[7] According to this theory, a city that is losing its middle class, upper-middle class, and affluent population is failing, since it's unable to provide the public goods, services, and amenities preferred by members of these groups.

But we also know that factors out of the control of city officials and voters matter as well. This means that any analysis of a city's decline needs to consider not only political institutions, fiscal policy, and regulatory policy but also outside factors, such as people's preference for a pleasant climate, regional economic shocks, and path dependency. In the following chapters and in light of the economic theories just discussed, we will examine the story of one American city's rise, decline, and transition from an industrial powerhouse to a city still looking for an identity in the modern economy.

---

6. US Census Bureau, "US Cities Are Home to 62.7 Percent of the US Population, but Comprise Just 3.5 Percent of the Land Area," March 4, 2015, https://www.census.gov/newsroom/press-releases/2015/cb15-33.html.

7. Charles M. Tiebout, "A Pure Theory of Local Expenditures," *Journal of Political Economy* 64, no. 5 (October 1956): 416–24.

CHAPTER 2

Dayton from the Turn of the Twentieth Century to 1930

A PERIOD OF OPTIMISM

> Dayton is a city of buoyancy and responsiveness. Its present population is estimated about 175,000. A forecast of future growth, based upon carefully worked out methods which are believed to be generally reliable, indicates that by the year 1970 Dayton's population should approach 400,000.
>
> —DAYTON CHAMBER OF COMMERCE AND DAYTON INDUSTRIAL ASSOCIATION, MAY 1, 1926[1]

DAYTON IS located along the Great Miami River in the Miami Valley region of Ohio, about 54 miles north of Cincinnati and the Ohio River by car and a little over 30 miles east of the Indiana border. Many large cities formed on the banks of rivers for several reasons, including access to drinking water and water power. It was also generally cheaper to move people and goods by water than over land. Cars, paved highways, and airplanes have since reduced the cost advantages of water travel, but the large amount of international shipping that still takes place on the oceans attests to the cost effectiveness of water transportation.

The city is named after Jonathan Dayton, a captain in the US military during the American Revolution and signer of the US Constitution. The first group of European settlers arrived in Dayton in 1796, and by 1800 a saw mill and a grist mill were in production.[2] Ohio was granted statehood in 1803, and Dayton was chosen as the county seat of the newly formed Montgomery County.

To get a sense of the size of the area's economy in those early years, total tax receipts for Montgomery County amounted to $373.96 in 1804 (equiva-

---

1. "Dayton as an Industrial City," Dayton Chamber of Commerce, Dayton History Books, May 1, 1926, http://www.daytonhistorybooks.com/page/page/1512274.htm.

2. History of Dayton, https://web.archive.org/web/20151112155224/http://www.cityofdayton.org/cco/Pages/BriefHistory.aspx.

lent to approximately $8,014 in 2017). In 1810 tax receipts for Montgomery County had increased to $1,644 (equivalent to approximately $33,806 in 2017).[3] The population of Dayton in 1810 was 323, while nearby Cincinnati had a population of 2,320.

By 1870 Dayton's population had grown to 30,000. Forty years later, its population had almost quadrupled to 116,000. It was during this period of robust growth at the turn of the twentieth century that Dayton showed an ability to adapt to widespread technological change. In the late 1800s Dayton was home to factories that produced iron plows, hay rakes, wooden boxes, pails, and wagons. In 1880 the Barney and Smith car company was one of the five largest producers of wooden rail cars in the country, and it employed 20% of all the industrial workers in Dayton.[4] But by 1910 many of the companies producing farm and rail equipment were gone. Even Barney and Smith was in receivership by 1913.[5] New factories producing cash registers, gasoline engines, and electric generators—products for a new, modern age—had taken their place.

The economic environment that fostered Dayton's robust, diverse, and innovative economy during this period did so by allowing entrepreneurs to thrive. It's tempting to attribute a city's success to the fact that certain accomplished and influential people made their homes there; think Henry Ford and Detroit. But people like Henry Ford who are capable of achieving success and changing the world can be found in any city. This is not to say that individuals don't have an impact—they obviously do—but what's really important is having the right institutions and policies in place that allow innovative people to maximize their potential. Creating a culture of innovation is the real key to urban success, and in the beginning of the twentieth century Dayton had such a culture. The result was a city full of successful people, but five in particular stand out due to their lasting contributions that affected Dayton—and the world—long after their deaths.

Readers familiar with Dayton's history will recognize these names, while even those unfamiliar with the history will recognize at least two. The following short biographies of John H. Patterson, Edward A. Deeds, Charles F. Kettering, and Orville and Wilbur Wright provide some insight into the economy of Dayton during its most innovative period and help establish a

---

3. Lawrence H. Officer and Samuel H. Williamson, "The Annual Consumer Price Index for the United States, 1774–Present," MeasuringWorth.com, 2018.

4. Judith Sealander, *Great Plans: Business Progressivism and Social Change in Ohio's Miami Valley 1890–1929* (Lexington: University of Kentucky Press, 1988), 18.

5. Sealander, *Great Plans*, 18.

connection between Dayton's past and its present, which is important for understanding the life of the city.

John H. Patterson

John Henry Patterson founded National Cash Register (NCR) with his brother in 1884. NCR, then simply referred to as "The Cash," became Dayton's largest employer by the early 1900s, and Patterson was perhaps the most influential man in Dayton until his death in 1922. He was the creator of several sales techniques still employed today, including the designated sales territory. He was also a proponent of progressive work policies and a demanding, eccentric boss who routinely fired his employees only to rehire them.[6] One example of his eccentricity is when Patterson fired his company's entire cost department by leading the employees to the company's boiler room and then tossing their accounting records into the coal furnace before dismissing them.[7] Patterson's influence over Dayton in the early 1900s was substantial, and he dominates the historical accounts of the city. His name appears often in this book as well.

Patterson was born in Dayton in 1844. His parents were farmers and like many farmers' children, Patterson's working career began on the family farm. In addition to his daily chores, he attended and completed both elementary school and high school in Dayton. He graduated in 1862 and then enrolled at Miami University in Oxford, Ohio. He attended Miami for only a year before returning home to run the farm after his father's death. The Civil War was raging by this time and shortly after he got back to Dayton he joined the Ohio volunteer infantry. John didn't see any active duty, and after being discharged in 1864, he enrolled at Dartmouth to finish the education he had started at Miami. He graduated in 1867, but without a job and with few prospects he returned to the family farm in Dayton.

Over the next year John performed many duties on the farm, including running the store and the stall at the Dayton market where his family sold their output.[8] While running the store, he often made accounting mistakes, either crediting or charging customers more than he should. His frustration

---

6. John R. Schleppi, "'It Pays': John H. Patterson and Industrial Recreation at the National Cash Register Company," *Journal of Sport History* 6, no. 3 (1979): 20–28.

7. Marcosson, *Colonel Deeds*, 74.

8. Samuel Crowther, *John H. Patterson: Pioneer in Industrial Welfare* (New York: Garden City Publishing Co., 1926), 30.

with bookkeeping may have helped him see the value of the cash register when others overlooked it.

His inability to find employment outside the family farm, particularly in the growing field of manufacturing, caused John to resent his college education. To him, it seemed as if the only thing a college degree was good for was being a lawyer, doctor, or clergyman, and he wasn't interested in any of those occupations. As a result, he reluctantly took a job as a toll collector on the portion of the Miami and Erie Canal that passed through Dayton.[9]

Like the collector he replaced, Patterson was required to live in the office to ensure he was available when a ship passed through. He soon discovered that collecting tolls was an infrequent and irregular business, which meant a lot of free time. He also realized that in the toll-collecting business there was little hope for advancement or a raise. As a result, he decided to open a side business selling and delivering coal and wood from his office to earn extra income.

Patterson soon turned his side business into his full-time job. He and his brother, Frank, eventually purchased their own coal fields to supply their delivery business, and over the next 15 years they did well. However, in 1881 a partnership with some Boston railroad executives went south and by 1884 he was out of the coal business. Patterson ultimately lost $24,000 and three years of work. This unsuccessful foray into business could have been another setback to what had been a rather ordinary career. Instead, it turned out to be a critical turning point.

Patterson had become acquainted with the cash register in 1882. As was common at the time, Patterson had established a store to sell goods to the miners of his coalfields. Once he began thinking about getting out of the coal business, he decided to closely examine the business's books to see what an appropriate sale price would be. It was then that he discovered that the clerks who ran his store often failed to charge for all the goods they sold. Patterson was irate and wanted some way to monitor his clerks that did not involve him being on site 24 hours a day. He had heard of a device, patented by Dayton saloonkeeper James Ritty, that could record a store's transactions, and he immediately sent for two of them. These cash registers were crude by today's standards, but they did the job.

Despite Patterson's endorsement, the cash register had largely been a dud up to that point. Inventor James Ritty couldn't sell them, and shortly after he began manufacturing them in 1879 he sold out to another business-

---

9. Crowther, *John H. Patterson*, 34.

man, J. H. Eckert. By 1884 when Patterson was exiting the coal business, only 50 registers had been sold and Patterson had bought four of them.

After he got out of the coal business, Patterson and his brother headed west to explore the idea of raising cattle. While they were in Colorado Springs, they met a merchant who told them he was on a long vacation. Patterson was intrigued by this, since his previous retail experience showed him that long absences from one's business resulted in missing money. When Patterson expressed his concern to the merchant, the merchant told him that he had bought registers made in Dayton to keep track of his sales, and each day the receipts were mailed to him so that he could check on his business. This experience convinced Patterson that the cash register could be a viable product.[10] Patterson and his brother gave up on the idea of ranching and returned to Dayton the next day.

J. H. Eckert had sold the cash register to the National Manufacturing Company, and when Patterson returned, he made a deal with the company's president, George Phillips, to buy his controlling interest for $6,500. Upon hearing of the deal, Patterson was ridiculed by his peers, who all thought the cash register was useless. This made Patterson have second thoughts, but Phillips refused to let him back out of the deal. Forced to forge ahead, he changed the company's name to National Cash Register and began improving the register and hiring and training sales agents. By the early 1890s, NCR was selling over 15,000 registers per year. NCR grew to over 6,000 employees under Patterson's leadership, and its headquarters and factories occupied over 100 acres near the east bank of the Great Miami River on Dayton's southern border. By the time Patterson died in 1922, NCR had sold approximately two million cash registers.

Unlike some other industrialists of his time, Patterson wasn't much of an inventor. In the early years of NCR he tinkered with the cash register and made some small improvements, but his lasting contributions to industry were in organization, advertising, and sales. Patterson was an innovator when it came to sales training.[11] He held sales conventions, established the exclusive territory, and standardized best practices, all of which stood in contrast to the typical practice of the day, which was basically to rely on the charisma of individual salesmen. Patterson believed salesmen were made, not born, and NCR's sales training reflected this. Many NCR salesmen went on to illustrious business careers of their own, including Thomas Watson

10. Jon M. Hawes and John H. Patterson, "Leaders in Selling and Sales Management: John H. Patterson," *Journal of Personal Selling & Sales Management* 5, no. 2 (1985): 59–61.

11. Walter A. Friedman, "John H. Patterson and the Sales Strategy of the National Cash Register Company, 1884 to 1922," *Business History Review* 72, no. 4 (1998): 552–84.

Sr., who had been fired by Patterson but who later founded International Business Machines (IBM) and promoted Patterson's sales and management techniques.

Edward A. Deeds and Charles Kettering

Two of Patterson's NCR employees, Edward Deeds and Charles Kettering, became friends while working at the company, and they would later use this friendship as a foundation for a very successful business relationship. Edward Deeds moved to Dayton in 1897 after graduating from Denison College (now Denison University) with a degree in engineering.[12] He was particularly interested in electricity, a passion he shared with the man who would become his frequent collaborator, Charles Kettering. Deeds's first job in Dayton was as an installer and repairman for the Thresher Electric Company. Within two years he became the company's superintendent and chief engineer.

In 1899 he was hired away from Thresher by NCR. NCR wanted to electrify its manufacturing plant and hired Deeds to complete the job after the previous engineer was forced to retire due to illness. Deeds successfully electrified the plant and rose rapidly within the company. In 1903 he became assistant general manager in charge of engineering and construction. It was around this time that he first met Charles Kettering.[13]

Deeds's position brought him into contact with NCR's inventions department and on one of his visits he began studying the crank used to operate the cash registers. He thought that the crank could be replaced by an electric motor, but after devising a rough prototype he realized that he did not have the time to fully immerse himself in the project. His search for someone who had the ability and time led him to recent Ohio State University graduate Charles Kettering. Deeds hired Kettering in 1904, and Kettering soon perfected the electric motor for the cash register.

Kettering and Deeds formed a fast friendship, and Deeds continued to move up the ladder at NCR. In 1910 he became vice president and assistant general manager of the entire company. Yet despite the success and enjoyment his work at NCR brought him, Deeds wasn't completely fulfilled. He believed there was money to be made in the automotive industry, and he was determined to get some of it.

---

12. Marcosson, *Colonel Deeds*, 60.
13. Marcosson, *Colonel Deeds*, 87.

One year before he became vice president, Deeds had approached Kettering about his desire to get involved with the auto industry, and together they cofounded the Dayton Engineering Laboratories Company (Delco).[14] Kettering left NCR almost right away to work at Delco full time, while Deeds initially only worked on Delco-related projects on nights and weekends. Finally, in 1915, Deeds retired from NCR to focus his energies on Delco. He would later rejoin NCR in 1931 as chief executive of the company.

While Edward Deeds was a successful inventor in his own right, Charles Kettering was the real genius. Kettering was only two years younger than Deeds, but an eye ailment delayed his college education and as a result he began his working career seven years after Deeds. Kettering distinguished himself as an inventor and engineer during his time at NCR. In addition to his perfection of the electric motor used to power NCR's cash registers, he developed a mechanism that enabled cash registers to subtract and he devised a credit approval system that made it easy for merchants to extend credit to customers.

But his greatest inventions were in the automotive industry. Together with Deeds and other engineers poached from NCR's inventions department—collectively known as the "Barn Gang" because they worked in the barn behind Deeds's house—Kettering developed the first practical electric self-starter for cars. Early cars were started by hand using a crank that required a significant amount of strength. Cars of the time often stalled too, and this frequent stalling combined with the strength needed to restart them made it impossible for anyone who lacked the required strength to drive alone. The crank could also cause injuries if the engine kicked back during the cranking process; it was not uncommon for the starting of a car to result in a broken arm, strained back, or broken jaw. Kettering's electric starter eliminated these problems.

The first car to use Kettering's starter was the 1912 Cadillac. The 1912 Cadillac also had an electric lighting system powered by the same small electric motor that started the car. Headlights had previously been powered by compressed acetylene gas. The electric starter was a big success and soon spread to other carmakers. Interestingly, one of the last cars to employ the starter was Ford's Model T, which used a hand crank until 1919.

Unlike Deeds, who returned to NCR to serve as its CEO in 1931, Kettering remained in the automotive industry for the rest of his career. In 1916 Delco was bought by United Motors, and it was here that Kettering first met the future president of General Motors, Alfred Sloan. United Motors,

---

14. Marcosson, *Colonel Deeds,* 114.

and thus Delco, was bought by GM in 1918. One year later GM purchased all the companies owned by Kettering and Deeds—Dayton Metal Products Company, Dayton Wright Airplane Company, and the Domestic Engineering Company—primarily to obtain the complete attention and talents of Kettering.[15] Delco became a large supplier of parts for GM vehicles, including ignition and lighting systems.

In 1920 the General Motors Research Corporation was established at Kettering's laboratories in Moraine, just south of Dayton. In 1925 the Research Corporation was moved to Detroit. Kettering remained in charge of GM Research until his retirement in 1947.[16] In addition to the electric starter, Kettering developed nontoxic coolants for refrigerators, leaded gasoline, and high-compression engines, among many other things.[17] By the time of his death in 1958, Kettering had organized and operated five research laboratories in the Dayton area.[18]

The Wright Brothers

Ohio's license plate refers to the state as the birthplace of aviation, and this well-deserved epithet is due to the work of Orville and Wilbur Wright, collectively known as the Wright brothers. Despite their close association with Dayton, only the younger brother, Orville, was born there in 1871. Wilbur was born in Millville, Indiana, four years earlier. After spending most of their childhood years in Iowa and Indiana due to their father's position as a reverend in the United Brethren Church, Wilbur, Orville, and the rest of the Wright family permanently settled in Dayton in 1884. At the time Wilbur was 17 and Orville was 13, yet despite their advanced ages both would come to consider Dayton their hometown. In fact, after he had become famous for his airplane, Wilbur remarked, when asked about how to get ahead in

---

15. In regards to GM's purchase of the companies owned by Kettering, Alfred Sloan reports "that Mr. Charles F. Kettering . . . is the center of this situation; that the obtaining of Mr. Kettering's entire time and attention is of the prime importance, it being desired to place him in charge of the new Detroit laboratory . . . and that in the opinion of Mr. Durant, Mr. Haskell, Mr. Sloan, Mr. Chrysler and others Mr. Kettering is by far the most valuable man known to this Corporation for the position." Alfred Pritchard Sloan, *My Years with General Motors*, ed. John McDonald and Catharine Stevens (New York: Doubleday, 1963), 73.

16. Sloan, *My Years*, 250.

17. Sloan, *My Years*, 93.

18. T. A. Boyd, "The Charles F. Kettering Archives," *Technology and Culture* 5, no. 3 (1964): 412–15.

life, that one should "Pick out a good father and mother and begin life in Ohio."[19]

The brothers were known to be inseparable, and together they shared all their successes and failures. Their first business venture together was as printers. They published various versions of their own paper and did printing jobs for others, including a short-lived weekly paper for Dayton's black community edited by Orville's friend and high school classmate Paul Laurence Dunbar.[20]

The brothers were in the printing business from 1889 to 1892, but in the spring of 1893, they shifted gears in response to a new sensation that was sweeping the country, the bicycle. The brothers sold and repaired bicycles for a couple years in two different shops on West Third Street, about a block north of their house on Hawthorn Street. In 1895 they moved for a third time to a building on South Williams Street, a smaller street just off Third. This shop had a showroom downstairs at street level and a machine shop upstairs. It was here they began building their own bicycle, which they named the Van Cleve in honor of their great-great-grandmother. Business continued to grow, and in 1897 they moved for the last time to a still larger location back on West Third Street. This last location is the most famous shop, and it was taken down brick by brick and moved to Dearborn, Michigan—along with the Wrights' home on Hawthorn Street—by Henry Ford in 1936–37 for his outdoor museum, where it can still be viewed today. The shop on South Williams Street is still in Dayton and today it's part of the Dayton Aviation Heritage Park.

It was in the final shop on West Third Street that the brothers began to think seriously about how to solve the problem of flight. Several other parties from all over the world, including the French government; Samuel Langley, scientist and head of the Smithsonian Institution; and successful American inventors Alexander Graham Bell and Thomas Edison, were also trying to create a practical flying machine. But it was the Wright brothers—without any formal education, outside financing, connections, or government subsidies—who would finally succeed.[21]

The Wright brothers recognized that the key to controlled flight was identical to that of riding a bike—maintaining equilibrium. Flying machines of the time largely relied on the pilot shifting his weight to maintain bal-

---

19. David McCullough, *The Wright Brothers* (New York: Simon and Schuster, 2015), 12.

20. McCullough, *Wright Brothers*, 19.

21. Philip N. Johnson-Laird, "Flying Bicycles: How the Wright Brothers Invented the Airplane," *Mind & Society* 4, no. 1 (2005): 27–48.

ance—like one does on a bicycle—but this was ineffective in the air. Through his observations of birds, Wilbur realized that birds in flight maintain stability by tilting their wings so that they cut the wind at different angles as necessary. The brothers realized that a plane would require a similar capability in order to be controlled. Their idea of "wing warping" was their first important and original contribution to the advancement of powered flight.[22]

The brothers' first machines were manned gliders, which they famously tested at Kitty Hawk, North Carolina, for several weeks each year between 1900 and 1902.[23] Kitty Hawk provided the sustained winds necessary for takeoff and sand that cushioned their landings. During this time, they discovered that practically all the published data about the correct curvature of wings and other aspects of flying were wrong. There had been such little success flying even manned gliders that no one had been able to correctly calculate the lift and drag ratios needed to sustain a manned aircraft.

The brothers approached this problem by building a small-scale wind tunnel in their shop in Dayton. Despite their lack of formal scientific training, they conducted many rigorous experiments using old hacksaw blades cut and hammered into different wing shapes. *The Aeronautical Journal of the Aeronautical Society of Great Britain* would later write, "Never in the history of the world had men studied the problem with such scientific skill nor with such undaunted courage."[24]

By 1903 the brothers had learned enough from their gliders and wind tunnel to attempt a powered flight. Their friend and shop employee Charlie Taylor built a four-cylinder engine to power their flyer. The engine along with the rest of the flyer was shipped to Kitty Hawk in pieces in the fall of 1903, where Orville and Wilbur reassembled it. By mid-December, after a few setbacks due to broken parts, the flyer was fully assembled and ready for takeoff. On December 14, with Wilbur in control thanks to a coin toss, the brothers launched their flyer.[25] Everything worked perfectly except that Wilbur pulled up too hard upon takeoff and then overcorrected, causing the flyer to crash.

The necessary repairs were made and three days later, on December, 17, 1903, it was finally Orville's turn. Orville's first flight, and the first ever suc-

22. McCullough, *Wright Brothers,* 38.

23. G. D. Padfield and B. Lawrence, "The Birth of Flight Control: An Engineering Analysis of the Wright Brothers' 1902 Glider," *Aeronautical Journal* 107, no. 1078 (December 2003): 697–718.

24. McCullough, *Wright Brothers,* 70.

25. Orville Wright, *"How We Made the First Flight,"* Department of Transportation, Federal Aviation Administration, Office of General Aviation Affairs, 1977.

cessful controlled flight in a heavier-than-air flying machine, covered 120 feet and lasted about 12 seconds. Later that day Wilbur would fly over 800 feet during a flight lasting nearly one minute.

Over the next five years the Wright brothers improved their flying machine but did so closer to home to cut expenses. They practiced just outside Dayton at Huffman Prairie, a field they rented from a local farmer. Today the field is part of Wright-Patterson Air Force Base. To make up for Ohio's lack of consistent wind, the brothers created a launching device that dropped a heavy weight to propel their flyer forward. A similar technology is used to launch jets on aircraft carriers today.

By 1904 they were flying in circles and S-shaped patterns. In October 1905 in their new 25-horsepower Flyer III, Wilbur flew for over 38 minutes, landing only when he ran out of gas.[26] This was longer than all their other flights combined.

The brothers wanted to capitalize on their machine and contacted several governments about purchasing a flyer. They were routinely rebuffed, many believing their feats impossible despite growing newspaper coverage and hundreds of witnesses. They finally made a deal with the French government in 1908, and Wilbur went to France to demonstrate the flyer's capabilities and to train some French pilots.

His demonstrations made him an instant celebrity. Both brothers had become proficient pilots, and Wilbur's ability to bank and turn in midair amazed everyone who saw him fly. Politicians, millionaires, and even kings came to France to watch Wilbur pilot his flyer. The US government had also become interested by this time, and Orville performed similar feats at Fort Myer in Arlington, Virginia, next to Arlington National Cemetery. Together they made Dayton an internationally recognized city. After their successful demonstrations, the brothers started the Wright Company in 1909 to manufacture airplanes and protect their intellectual property.

Unfortunately, the brothers were not able to fly as much as they would have liked in the years to follow. They spent much of that time securing their achievement as the inventors of the airplane and fighting patent infringement lawsuits, all of which they eventually won.[27] Wilbur died unexpectedly in 1912 of typhoid fever, and left most of his estate to Orville, who continued to be involved with the airplane and aviation in general. Orville sold the Wright Company in 1915 and established the Wright Aeronautical Laboratory to concentrate on his scientific research. Orville's longer life and the

26. McCullough, *Wright Brothers,* 127.

27. Herbert A. Johnson, "The Wright Patent Wars and Early American Aviation," *Journal of Air Law and Commerce* 69, no. 1 (2004): 21.

financial success of the Wright Company made him a wealthy man, worth an estimated $10 million in today's dollars at the time of his death. This is a significant sum but perhaps not as much as one would expect considering the financial potential of the airplane. Orville lived to see many aeronautical achievements made possible by his and Wilbur's groundbreaking work, including Charles Lindbergh's historic flight and the first jet aircraft. He died of a heart attack at Dayton's Miami Valley Hospital in 1948.

Culture of Innovation

All these entrepreneurs impacted Dayton's economy for many decades after their deaths. In the Wright brothers' case, their work continues to have a large effect on Dayton's economy through Wright-Patterson Air Force Base. The base began as Wilbur Wright Field, which was established as a World War I pilot training ground in 1917 just outside Dayton and included Huffman Prairie, where the brothers had mastered the art of flying. In 1924 the city of Dayton purchased the field along with other nearby land and named it Wright Field. Boeing and other companies used it as a testing field during the interwar years before the US military once again used it as an air force base in World War II. After the war, the base was renamed Wright-Patterson Air Force Base in honor of the Wright brothers and Lt. Frank Patterson, a World War I pilot and the nephew of NCR founder John Patterson. Today Wright-Patterson is the Dayton area's largest employer, with over 27,000 military, civilian, and contract employees.[28]

Like the Wright brothers, entrepreneurs Patterson, Deeds, and Kettering were able to thrive in Dayton's culture of innovation. The companies they created—notably NCR and Delco—were the major employers for tens of thousands of Dayton residents over the twentieth century. A later chapter will further discuss the role Kettering and Deeds played in turning Dayton into a hub of automobile-related manufacturing, but for now the important point is that these entrepreneurs created the companies that became the backbone of Dayton's economy over the ensuing decades.

And while these five were the most influential of Dayton's entrepreneurs during this period, they were not the only sources of innovation. A broader indication of Dayton's culture of innovation in the beginning of the twentieth century can be found in patent data from the period. In 1900 Dayton generated nearly 12 patents per 10,000 people, a rate that placed it first in a

---

28. Joe Cogliano, "Wright-Patterson Air Force Base Economic Impact Tops $5B," August 14, 2010, https://www.bizjournals.com/dayton/stories/2010/08/09/daily44.html?surround=lfn.

sample of 35 large US cities that included Boston, New York, Philadelphia, Detroit, Cincinnati, and Cleveland.[29] In 1910 Dayton generated a similar number of patents per 10,000 people and was ranked third on the same list, behind Worcester and Lynn, Massachusetts.[30]

The importance of innovation and entrepreneurship to economic growth has long been known. In his book, *Capitalism, Socialism and Democracy*, economist Joseph Schumpeter used the term "creative destruction" to describe how entrepreneurs generate new and better products and technologies that supplant or destroy old ones, increasing output and living standards in the process.[31] In *The Economy of Cities*, urbanist Jane Jacobs describes cities as places where new work is created out of old work.[32] The large amount of people in cities enables more specialization and exchange of not only goods and services but knowledge as well. The proximity of people in cities increases the opportunities for human interaction, which quickens the transmission of ideas and information. This aggregation of specialized knowledge, along with the rapid dissemination of information, fosters further innovation as entrepreneurs identify and act on unexploited profit opportunities. A city's success is directly related to its ability to innovate and generate new ideas, and cities devoid of entrepreneurs who generate new, innovative ideas will stagnate and decay.

As the previous profiles and patent data show, Dayton didn't suffer from a lack of new ideas in the early decades of the twentieth century. In fact, the 1920s was a time of great optimism for the people of Dayton, as the quote discussing future population growth at the beginning of this chapter indicates. This optimism was due to the robust growth the city was experiencing and the confidence that stemmed from solving a large collective-action problem several years earlier that had threatened the city's future.

The Great Dayton Flood

Due in large part to the economic opportunities provided by entrepreneurs like Patterson, Kettering, Deeds, and the Wright brothers, Dayton's population and economy grew rapidly over the first two decades of the twentieth

29. Irwin Feller, "The Urban Location of United States Invention, 1860–1910," *Explorations in Economic History* 8, no. 3 (1971): 285–303.

30. Feller, "Urban Location," 294. Lynn was the home of Thomson-Houston Electric Company, a precursor to General Electric.

31. Joseph A. Schumpeter, *Capitalism, Socialism and Democracy* (London: Routledge, 2013).

32. Jane Jacobs, *The Economy of Cities* (New York: Vintage, 1970).

century: From 1900 to 1920 the city's population grew by 79%. But while growth was strong, the city had a recurring problem that had the potential to curtail future growth if left unaddressed—flooding.

Throughout its history, Dayton's location in the Miami Valley made it susceptible to periodic flooding. Carved out by retreating glaciers, the Miami Valley is approximately 120 miles long and varies in width from a quarter mile to three miles. The Great Miami River is the main river running through the area and it feeds into the Ohio River. The entire Miami River watershed covers more than 3,900 square miles.

The Great Miami River divides Dayton's east and west sides, and near the downtown area of the city three other rivers feed into it: Mad River, Stillwater River, and Wolf Creek. The confluence of these four rivers made the city's downtown susceptible to flooding during periods of heavy rain. By the time of the Great Flood in 1913, the inhabitants of Dayton were familiar with flooding. The first recorded flood in the area occurred in March 1805, and it was followed by several other notable floods throughout the nineteenth century. Recorded floods occurred in 1814, 1828, 1832, 1847, 1866, 1883, 1897, and 1898. Prior to the 1913 flood, the 1866 flood resulted in the most damage, approximately $250,000 (around $4 million in today's dollars). Dayton and the surrounding towns in the Miami Valley region responded to each flood with progressively higher levees, but there was no region-wide, systemic solution in place to deal with the frequent flooding.[33] This would soon change.

In March 1913 several weather events united to create the ideal conditions for a massive flood. Three weather systems—one that originated in the Gulf of Mexico, another at the mouth of the St. Lawrence River in Canada, and a third that formed in the northern Great Plains—joined together just above Dayton. Once merged, the entire weather system stretched from Indianapolis, Indiana to Columbus, Ohio, a distance of 176 miles.

Niagara Falls discharges 1,590,000 gallons of water per second. At that rate it would take nearly 28 days to discharge the amount of water that fell on the region.

The rain that ultimately caused the flood began on Easter Sunday, March 23, 1913. On the morning of March 24 the staff of the US Weather Bureau in Dayton realized that the lowlands in the area were likely to flood so they made phone calls to the residents of those areas to warn them of the high probability of flooding. In the early evening all on-duty members of the

---

33. Arthur Ernest Morgan, *The Miami Conservancy District* (New York: McGraw-Hill, 1951), 17.

Dayton Police Department went door to door in the lower levels of the city and urged people to seek higher ground. Not long after, major portions of the city were under as much as 20 feet of water.

From March 23 to March 27 approximately nine inches of rain fell on 2,500 square miles of land. The total amount of water was 3.9 trillion gallons, which is enough water to fill a 25-square-mile hole that's 25 feet deep.[34] To make matters worse, the area had previously experienced several lighter periods of rain that had left the ground saturated. This meant that most of the rain left the area as runoff, flowing into nearby streams, gullies, and rivers. And since it was only early spring, the air temperature was low and the evaporation rate was slow.

The flood wiped out most telegraph lines, which made communication with other cities difficult. The organization responsible for much of the immediate flood relief was internal—the Dayton Citizens' Relief Association (DCRA). However, immediately prior to the flood this organization didn't exist. Instead, it was NCR, the largest producer of cash registers in the United States and the largest privately owned company in Dayton. On the morning of March 24, from his company's headquarters located on high ground just south of downtown Dayton, NCR's founder and president John H. Patterson presciently recognized the disaster that was about to befall Dayton.

Patterson's entrepreneurial spirit and management skills turned out to be an important asset for the city of Dayton, even outside of the contributions his company made to the local economy. In the early morning of Tuesday, March 25, Patterson presided over a meeting attended by most of NCR's top executives. In a span of 15 minutes he turned his entire 7,000-employee organization into a relief agency focused on providing emergency services for the people of Dayton. Later that same day, Dayton mayor Edward Phillips declared NCR the flood relief headquarters of the city.[35]

NCR's commissary team was put in charge of food and told to bake bread and prepare soup. The hydraulics team was put in charge of maintaining NCR's pumping station and wells to ensure that clean drinking water was available. The purchasing team was ordered to send trucks and wagons to the surrounding areas and purchase food items, cots, beds, blankets, clothing, shoes, hats, gloves, etc. for the people whose belongings would soon be destroyed. The communications team was responsible for alerting mayors, fire departments, police departments, and other civic leaders in

---

34. Allan W. Eckert, *A Time of Terror: The Great Dayton Flood* (Santa Fe, NM: Landfall Press, 1965), 4.

35. Eckert, *Time of Terror*, 89.

every principal city in the area about the impending flood. The medical team was ordered to gather aspirin, iodine, bandages, and other medical supplies to provide first aid to the flood victims. Members of the team were also sent out to ask the doctors and nurses of the local hospitals to report to NCR if possible to staff the two emergency rooms, an isolation ward, a nursery, and a maternity ward. Patterson also set up a morgue and requested that the city coroner report to NCR.

The sanitation team was told to gather as much disinfectant as could be found and to ensure that the NCR sanitation system remained in working order. The security and fire team were ordered to provide basic security around the factory and to prevent theft and looting. A fire brigade that conducted regular fire patrols was also formed. The transportation team was responsible for organizing the vehicles and drivers that were to act as runners and gather supplies. The woodworking team was responsible for constructing wooden rescue boats. The safety personnel were told to form rescue teams to help move people in especially dangerous situations to safer ones and to take marooned residents to higher ground. And finally, the electrical team was ordered to transfer NCR's electric service to the emergency generators in anticipation of Dayton's electricity going out.[36]

The final layout of the DCRA inside of building 10 on the NCR campus was: first floor, food service; second floor, relief operations and military headquarters; third floor, general hospital; fourth floor, maternity ward and nursery; fifth through seventh floors, sleeping areas for men; eighth floor, barbers, cleaners, and other services; tenth and eleventh floors, women's sleeping areas. Historian Allan Eckert wrote:

> In one day the NCR had become a city unto itself: in the basement clothing salvaged from the flood was being disinfected, cleaned, and dried. Three women from the Services Department tacked up hastily lettered signs throughout the building, telling people where to go to get food and clothing, medical service, comfortable beds, freshly brewed coffee and even emergency dental service. A few reporters from the closer cities— Columbus, Cincinnati, Xenia, Lebanon, Springfield—began to show up and were provided with desks, typewriters, and cots on the second floor.[37]

On March 25 approximately 3,000 meals were served by the workers at NCR. The NCR woodworking team constructed approximately 200 wooden

---

36. Eckert, *Time of Terror*, 33.
37. Eckert, *Time of Terror*, 108.

boats and by 6:00 p.m. on Thursday, March 27 the boats had been used to transport approximately 4,600 people to dry land.

The 1913 flood caused over $1.5 billion in damage (adjusted for inflation) and killed 361 people.[38] This flood was terribly tragic, but the response is a great example of bottom-up disaster relief, as exemplified by the actions of John Patterson. Economist Emily Skarbek defines a system of bottom-up disaster relief as a system in which individuals create and enforce the rules that govern disaster relief for their own community.[39] The bottom-up nature of the system means that decisions about the administration of aid are made by individuals at the local level. In a top-down approach, there is one overarching authority and the lower levels of authority derive their authority from the individuals above them in the chain of command. This approach is common today. In America, the Federal Emergency Management Agency, or FEMA, often takes the lead, and state and local organizations play secondary roles.

Bottom-up disaster relief is more effective when fewer people have decision-making authority and when those people have a vested interest in the outcome. These conditions were met in Dayton. Patterson was the main decision maker during the height of the disaster. He employed his own company's resources to provide aid, which meant he had complete control of their use. Patterson also had strong familial and community ties to Dayton: He was born there in 1844 and founded his company there 1884. By 1913 he had been living in Dayton for 69 years and had been in business for 29 years.

Disasters are extreme situations and often decisions about distributing aid are made quickly and based on a relatively small amount information. The usual external signals of prices, profit, and loss that firms use to guide their behavior are often unavailable in these situations. Since these signals are lacking, the effectiveness of disaster relief is more susceptible to leadership quality. Patterson's longstanding ties to the area, his reputation as a successful businessman, and the fact that he was using his own personal resources meant that he had a strong incentive to see that the aid was effective and economically efficient. His actions during the flood saved thousands of lives, and Patterson was widely proclaimed a hero.

The Miami Conservancy District (MCD), the nation's first regional, coordinated effort at flood control, was created as a direct result of the 1913

---

38. Arthur E. Morgan, *The Miami Valley and the 1913 Flood: Technical Reports, Part 1* (Miami Conservancy District: Dayton, 1917). The amount of damage in 1913 was $67 million.

39. Emily C. Skarbek, "The Chicago Fire of 1871: A Bottom-Up Approach to Disaster Relief," *Public Choice* 160, no. 1–2 (July 2014): 155–80.

flood. As mentioned earlier, the typical response to previous floods had been to build larger levees, but now the people of Dayton wanted a more lasting solution. An initial survey of the area to be protected and the creation of an appropriate flood prevention plan was funded with two million dollars privately raised from 23,000 donors, which is an indicator of the idea's popularity. A law allowing the formation of a legal district to purchase the required property, issue bonds, and levy taxes was shepherded though the Ohio legislature by Dayton citizens such as Edward Deeds and former Ohio governor James Cox. The Conservancy Act of Ohio became law in March 1914 and the Miami Conservancy District was officially formed in June 1915.[40] Edward Deeds paid for the construction of a building in Dayton's downtown to serve as the MCD's headquarters, and it remains the headquarters today.[41] Deeds also served on the MCD's board of directors from 1915 to 1954.

Construction of the system did not start until 1918 and was completed in 1922.[42] The elaborate plan cost $34 million and involved constructing new roads and relocating railroad lines, houses, and even an entire town. The plan called for building five dry basins designed to store water during periods of heavy rain. Each basin has a dam that controls the release of water so as not to overwhelm the area's natural drainage system.

The town of Osborn was located within one of the proposed basins and as a result the entire town was purchased by the Miami Conservancy District and relocated two miles away, adjacent to the nearby city of Fairfield. The two cities eventually merged and became Fairborn. The basin and dam that led to Osborn's relocation is named the Huffman Dam (it's located near Huffman Prairie) and is a 15-minute drive from where I grew up.

The Miami Conservancy District was not only a feat of engineering but also a successful experiment in the provision of public goods.[43] Public goods are goods that don't dissipate with use and that are difficult to prevent people from using once they're created. It's often difficult to provide these goods privately since once they are created anyone can use them without contributing to their creation—or free ride—which gives people an incentive to take advantage of the work of others. And since everyone would rather

40. C. A. Bock, *History of the Miami Flood Control Project: Technical Reports*, pt. 2 (1918; repr., Ann Arbor: University of Michigan Library, 74).

41. "MCD Founders," Miami Conservancy District, accessed January 30, 2019, https://www.mcdwater.org/about-mcd-2/the-history-of-mcd/mcd-founders/.

42. "Construction," Miami Conservancy District, accessed January 30, 2019, https://www.mcdwater.org/about-mcd-2/the-history-of-mcd/construction/.

43. See J. Fred Giertz, "An Experiment in Public Choice: The Miami Conservancy District, 1913–1922," *Public Choice* 19, no. 1 (1974): 63–75.

have a free ride, too little of the public good gets produced. Flood protection is a great example of a public good since everyone benefits from it—even those who didn't contribute to its construction. The formation of the Miami Conservancy District enabled the citizens of the Miami Valley to overcome the free-rider problem.

The bonds used to fund the project were completely paid off in 1949 by taxes levied on Miami Valley residents in proportion to the increase in the value of their property as a result of the flood protection system. No federal or state aid was used in planning or constructing the project. Most importantly, since its completion the region has been flood-free. The regional flood system made people more confident about Dayton's future, and without it the city may never have achieved the size and success that it did.

The events of the Great Flood further demonstrate the importance of entrepreneurs to a city's success. John Patterson shepherded the city through the flood and the following cleanup with his quick decision making and the use of his own resources. Later, Edward Deeds used his resources and reputation to turn the Miami Conservancy District from a plan into a reality.[44] As these examples show, the leadership provided by successful private-sector entrepreneurs is often an asset in the public sector as well, and when that leadership is gone cities often struggle to fill the gap.

Industry in Dayton

With the Great Flood behind them and a capable prevention system in place, Dayton's many businesses were able to thrive. The Dayton of the 1920s prided itself on not being a "one-industry city." According to the Dayton Chamber of Commerce, Dayton was the US manufacturing leader in over 50 different commodities, including: cash registers, automobile lighting and ignition systems, electric refrigeration equipment, golf clubs, water softeners, and ice cream cones.[45] The manufacturing diversity of Dayton—along with its rising per-capita productivity, growing population, and relatively good government—gave city officials and residents many reasons to think that Dayton's best days were ahead.

In contrast to today, Dayton's geographic location was an asset in the early part of the twentieth century. As stated in Dayton Chamber of Commerce:[46]

---

44. Marcosson, *Colonel Deeds,* 185.
45. "Dayton as an Industrial City," Dayton History Books.
46. "Dayton as an Industrial City," Dayton History Books.

If one were able to select the best location in the United States for an industrial city of Dayton's type, the point selected would not be far from where
Dayton is now. Dayton lies 34 miles from the center of urban population of
the United States, 43 miles from the median point of total population, and
56 miles from the national center of manufactures.

Dayton had several waterways that could be used for shipping, most notably the Great Miami River, which connects to the Ohio River and enabled
trade down the Mississippi River and beyond during the city's early years.
The Miami and Erie Canal opened in 1829 and further increased Dayton's
ability to both export and import goods. By the middle of the nineteenth
century, railroads were the low-cost mode of transport and the importance
of navigable waterways declined. In terms of railroads, Dayton had "four
trunk line railroads, many trains to all major points, and . . . an excellence
of train service which would not be expected by one who had not made an
examination of the railroad maps and schedules." The Dayton Chamber of
Commerce concluded that, "Dayton has most favorable rail connections in
all directions."[47]

Due to its location and robust rail network, Dayton officials viewed the
city as the "hub of the wheel" with spokes connected by railroad to Chicago,
Detroit, New York, Cleveland, Buffalo, and Pittsburgh.[48] Each of these cities
was also thriving during the early twentieth century, and Dayton's strategic
position made it a national distribution center. In 1923 approximately 90%
of Dayton's $250 million worth of manufactured goods were exported out
of the city. International exports totaled 4.5% of output, which was a larger
percentage of output than the Ohio average.[49]

Dayton's taxes in this period were generally considered to be favorable.
As late as 1926 Ohio had no income tax and the Chamber of Commerce
described the state franchise tax levied on corporations as "not heavy."[50]
State license taxes and other local miscellaneous taxes were deemed fair as
well. The one complaint was that both real and personal property were taxed
at the same rate by the state, but in effect this was not a large issue since it

---

47. "Facts about Dayton: Preliminary Statement," Dayton Chamber of Commerce,
Dayton History Books, May 1, 1926, http://www.daytonhistorybooks.com/page/
page/1512266.htm.

48. "Facts about Dayton," Dayton Chamber of Commerce.

49. "Facts about Dayton," Dayton Chamber of Commerce.

50. "Facts about Dayton," Dayton Chamber of Commerce.

was rarely enforced. Other than that, Ohio's tax practices were described as "reasonable and normal."[51]

The City Manager in Dayton

Even though Dayton's tax policy was largely satisfactory during this period, there were some issues that city reformers wanted to address, particularly the influence of political machines and bosses. As a result, Dayton became a pioneer in municipal government in 1913 when—despite intense opposition from Democrats and the local Socialist Party—the citizens of Dayton adopted a charter that instituted a city-manager form of government to replace their mayor-council government.[52] The charter was approved by a two-to-one margin and went into effect on January 1, 1914.[53]

The city-manager form of government was introduced in Staunton, Virginia, in 1908.[54] Staunton was much smaller than Dayton at the time. In fact, when Dayton adopted the city-manager form of government it was the largest city to do so up to that point. The adoption of the city-manager plan in Dayton was enabled by a 1912 Ohio State constitutional amendment that extended a large measure of home rule to Ohio's municipalities. The amendment grants cities the privilege to adopt and enforce within their limits regulations concerning police, fire protection, and public health so long as the regulations are not in conflict with the general laws of the state.[55]

John H. Patterson of NCR and other members of Dayton's business community seized this opportunity to reform what they thought was an inefficient and corrupt government. Dayton's transition to a city-manager government brought it national attention. The plan was commonly referred to as the "Dayton Plan," and by 1919 more than 130 cities around the country had adopted variants of it.[56]

---

51. "Facts about Dayton," Dayton Chamber of Commerce.

52. Chester Edward Rightor, Don Conger Sowers, and Walter Matscheck, *City Manager in Dayton: Four Years of Commission-Manager Government, 1914–1917; and Comparisons with Four Preceding Years Under the Mayor-Council Plan, 1910–1913* (New York: Macmillan, 1919), 14.

53. Rightor, Sowers, and Matscheck, *City Manager*, 16.

54. James E. Rauch, "Bureaucracy, Infrastructure, and Economic Growth: Evidence from US Cities during the Progressive Era," *American Economic Review* 85, no. 4 (February 1995): 968–79.

55. Rightor, Sowers, and Matscheck, *City Manager*, 5.

56. James Weinstein, "Organized Business and the City Commission and Manager Movements," *Journal of Southern History* 28, no. 2 (May 1962): 166–82.

The city-manager government was strongly supported by many local business owners, but no one was as supportive as Patterson. To Patterson a city was "a great business enterprise whose stockholders are the people."[57] Patterson stated that a city should be directed "not by partisans, either Republican or Democratic, but by men who are skilled in business management and social science; who would treat our money as a trust fund, to be expended wisely and economically, without waste, and for the benefit of all citizens."[58] This was a commonly held view, particularly among business owners, and makes sense in light of the advances being made in industrial organization during this period. Like other successful business owners of this era, Patterson oversaw a firm that contained several departments and employed thousands of workers, all united toward a common goal. Firms of such size and complexity had become more prevalent than in the past, and it was natural for business owners to conclude that the processes they had created to successfully operate large, complex firms could also be used to operate large, complex cities.

The structure of the city-manager government in Dayton consists of five commissioners elected in nonpartisan, city-wide elections, who then appoint a city manager to execute the policies authorized by the commissioners. In short, the commission is responsible for policy while the city manager is responsible for performance. Figure 2 depicts the structure of the city-manager form of government and compares it to that of the factory. This figure exemplifies the commonly held view among contemporaneous supporters of city-manager government that the city and the factory/firm were analogous.[59]

As shown in figure 2, both the firm and city get their authority from the "owners" of the enterprise. In the case of the firm, it is the shareholders who actually own the firm in proportion to their investment, while in the case of the city it is the residents, who though they pay taxes do not individually own any of the city's property or assets. Both groups have ways of expressing their satisfaction or displeasure with management. Shareholders can vote or divest their financial interest while residents can vote; initiate referendums, recalls, and initiatives; protest; or move.

Both shareholders and residents delegate some authority to a governing body—the board of directors or the commissioners—which then chooses

---

57. John Patterson, "What Dayton, Ohio Should Do to Become a Model City," 1896, http://www.daytonhistorybooks.com/page/page/4390483.htm.

58. Patterson, "What Dayton, Ohio Should Do to Become a Model City."

59. Rightor, Sowers, and Matscheck, *City Manager,* 19.

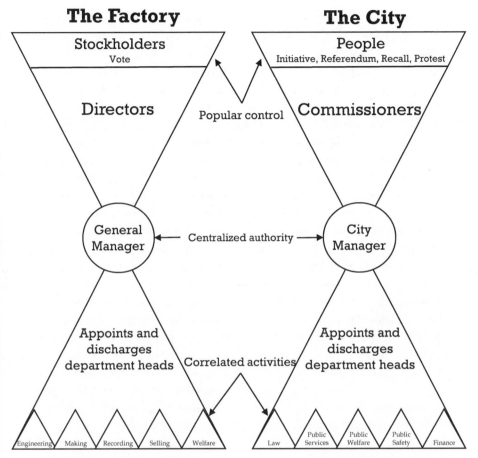

The Factory # The City

Stockholders
Vote

People
Initiative, Referendum, Recall, Protest

Directors Popular control **Commissioners**

General Manager ← Centralized authority → **City Manager**

Appoints and discharges department heads

Correlated activities

Appoints and discharges department heads

Engineering / Making / Recording / Selling / Welfare

Law / Public Services / Public Welfare / Public Safety / Finance

FIGURE 2. Several Dayton civic leaders and business owners believed that the organizational structure of the factory could be successfully transferred to the city. (Based on a diagram by Detroit Bureau of Governmental Research Inc. in Rightor, Sowers, and Matscheck, *City Manager*, 19.)

an executive to run the day-to-day operations. The general manager and city manager are responsible for achieving the objectives authorized by the board of directors and the city commissioners respectively, and they have the authority to appoint and discharge their subordinates in pursuit of these objectives. The city manager—like the general manager—does not require any formal approval from the commission in regard to managing the city's workforce. And finally, both the general manager and the city manager can be dismissed by their respective governing body, which can in turn be dismissed by shareholders or residents.

City-manager governments tended to strengthen—and in some cases introduce—the institution of civil service in an effort to ensure that only the most capable people were hired for city government positions as exemplified by their performance on a civil service exam. In Dayton's case, the city-manager charter reformed and strengthened the corrupt civil service system that was already in place. Prior to the reforms, the commission that oversaw municipal hiring used an elaborate series of written symbols to indicate the applicant's political party, race, and probability of voting.[60] Applicants in the wrong party or of the wrong race could be denied employment. Also, applicants who were deemed unlikely to vote for the party were less likely to get a city job—party membership alone was not enough. This system allowed the party in power to maintain political patronage despite rules against it.

One explanation for why the business community was supportive of the city-manager plan in the early twentieth century is the increasing importance of government-provided goods and services as inputs in production; that is, the benefits of public and quasi-public goods had increased.[61] The automobile was becoming more widespread as a means of both travel and shipping, and this meant roads needed to be paved and maintained. Increasing urbanization caused by the rapid economic growth in cities also put pressure on other urban infrastructure such as water systems, sewage disposal, electricity generation, street lighting, railways, and fire stations and equipment. Businesspeople who lost productive workers to water-borne illnesses and unsanitary public spaces—a cost of ineffective government—lost a valuable input as well. John Patterson often stated that he supported public health projects and services because it paid to do so in the form of increased profits.[62] The business community saw how these services were being provided—or not provided—and concluded that the current institutional arrangements were preventing necessary improvements in the provision of government goods and services.

There is evidence from Dayton and across the country that the institutional reforms of the early twentieth century lowered the costs and improved the quality of government goods and services while also increasing economic activity. One study finds that during the Progressive Era, the institution of civil service had a positive effect on the share of city expenditures allocated to road and sewer infrastructure.[63] The study also finds that investments in roads, sewer, and water infrastructure increased manufacturing

---

60. Rightor, Sowers, and Matscheck, *City Manager,* 39.
61. Weinstein, "Organized Business," 167.
62. Sealander, *Great Plans,* 26.
63. Rauch, "Bureaucracy, Infrastructure," 14–15.

employment growth from 1904 to 1929. Thus, there is indirect evidence that the government reforms undertaken in Dayton—particularly the reforms to the civil service system—positively contributed to Dayton's economy by stimulating growth in manufacturing.

There is also Dayton-specific evidence that the reforms successfully improved government-provided goods and services. One study finds that after five years of city-manager government in Dayton, "municipal garbage collection had been instituted, a municipal asphalt plant built, new sewers, based on the projected needs of 1950, constructed, parks improved, new bridges erected, trees planted, and a department of public welfare established."[64]

Another study published in 1919, shortly after the transition to city-manager government, also makes a compelling case on behalf of the reforms.[65] The study compares Dayton's government in the four years preceding reform to the four years after reform along several dimensions. Costs were reduced in food inspection, garbage collection, and street cleaning, and the infant mortality rate fell, a result the authors attribute to improved milk inspections by the city.[66]

It's possible that cost reductions occurred in several other activities as well, such as ash and rubbish collection and road paving, but in these and other instances no records of costs were kept prior to the implementation of the city-manager government. This is evidence that consistent and accurate record keeping should also be viewed as another benefit of the city-manager government.

In addition to cost reductions, Dayton was able to increase the number of food and sanitation inspections, increase the pressure and availability of water, reduce street repair costs, consolidate and lower the cost of city purchases, decrease municipal debt, improve sanitation in the city's prison facilities and lower the cost of meals, and provide new services such as city nurses and legal aid—all with only a slight increase in the property tax rate.[67]

---

64. Weinstein, "Organized Business," 180

65. Rightor, Sowers, and Matscheck, *City Manager*, 127–204.

66. I mention all these outcomes merely to demonstrate the differences between pre- and post-reform government, not as an argument either for or against the government's provision of these goods and services.

67. Dayton itself had very little control over the local tax rate. Ohio State law limited the property taxes levied for state, county, school, township, and city purposes to 15 mills. A County Budget Commission was empowered to adjust tax rates to ensure that they complied with the law and cities had no representation on the commission, which often meant they received what was left over after the other entities had set their rates. See Rightor, Sowers, and Matscheck, *City Manager*, 173.

It seems reasonable to conclude that the city-manager form of government improved the production and delivery of government-provided goods
and services in Dayton in the early twentieth century. The infrastructure
improvements undertaken due to the reforms also positively impacted
subsequent growth in manufacturing. Additionally, political scientist Alan
DiGaetano shows that Dayton's transition to the city-manager form of government broke the political machines of Republican Joseph E. Lowes and
Democrat Edward Hanley and stymied the local Socialist Party.[68] Since governments run by political machines tend to be inefficient and corrupt and
socialism has generally reduced economic growth where it has been tried,
thwarting all three groups likely helped Dayton's economy at the time.

However, the modern evidence in favor of city managers versus other
forms of local government is less clear. One study uses data from the 1980s
and finds that city managers are no more efficient than mayor-council forms
of government.[69] Another separate study finds similar results.[70] On the other
hand, using data from 1995 to 2010, economist John Dove finds that city-
manager governments are associated with higher municipal bond ratings
and thus face a lower cost of borrowing.[71]

One possible reason for these contrasting findings is that the city-manager form of government has evolved over time. The aforementioned studies note that the differences between the city-manager and other forms of
government became much smaller in practice than in theory in the latter
half of the twentieth century. Mayors in city-manager governments today
take active roles in promoting policy and use their figurehead role to promote their views during official city functions. Even Dayton has a mayor
who is separately elected today, a change that was implemented in 1969.
Previously, the position of mayor did not have a separate political race—the
mayor was simply the chairperson of the five-member commission and had
no additional authority. Today the mayor of Dayton takes a more active role
in governing the city.

68. Alan DiGaetano, "Urban Political Reform:" Did It Kill the Machine?," *Journal of Urban History* 18, no. 1 (1991): 37–67.

69. Kathy Hayes and Semoon Chang, "The Relative Efficiency of City Manager and Mayor-Council Forms of Government," *Southern Economic Journal* 57, no. 1 (July 1990): 167–77.

70. Kevin T. Deno and Stephen L. Mehay, "Municipal Management Structure and Fiscal Performance: Do City Managers Make a Difference?," *Southern Economic Journal* 53, no. 3 (January 1987): 627–42.

71. John Dove, "Local Government Type and Municipal Bond Ratings: What's the Relationship?," *Applied Economics* 49, no. 24 (2017): 2339–51.

Dayton also moved away from actual nonpartisan elections. The race for mayor is still called nonpartisan, but the candidates are regularly described in the media as members of political parties and are regularly endorsed by local political parties.[72] The successful reform of government in Dayton in the early 1900s was in part due to reducing the role of politics in city management via actual nonpartisan elections and a nonpartisan city manager. These features are in effect no longer a part of the city-manager government in Dayton and may have reduced the city-manger government's effectiveness.

Moreover, early members of Dayton's commission were businesspeople first and politicians second. There was so much low-hanging fruit in terms of efficiency gains in the early years of reform that the commissioners—regardless of the party they identified with—largely agreed on what needed to be done. By the 1980s many of the best practices of municipal government—little patronage, centralized purchasing, accurate record keeping—had spread across the country, which made any differences between the efficiency of various forms of government relatively small. Additionally, the most overt forms of political corruption were eliminated in most cities by the latter half of the twentieth century, and this limited the opportunities for the city-manger form of government to improve city functions relative to the mayor-council form of government that had fostered many of the political machines.

The increasing role of the federal and state governments in the economy over the last 100 years has also reduced the role of city governments. As an example, Dayton's welfare department in the early 1900s conducted milk and food inspections, a task that today is done by the US Department of Agriculture. Other tasks have also been taken out of the hands of local officials and allocated to the federal and state governments, which has limited the opportunities for city governments to differentiate themselves. So while Dayton's reforms may have helped the city initially, there is less evidence that they gave the city a significant long-term advantage.

The first three decades of the twentieth century was an exciting time in Dayton. Dayton natives Wilbur and Orville Wright invented the first practical airplane, NCR dominated the cash-register market, and Edward Deeds and Charles Kettering began their foray into the automobile industry with the founding of Delco, which soon after became the catalyst for Dayton's

---

72. For a modern example, see Doug Page, "Whaley Entry in Race for Dayton Mayor Triggers Primary," *Dayton Daily News*, December 3, 2012, http://www.daytondailynews.com/news/news/whaley-to-seek-seat-for-dayton-mayor/nTLmP/.

decades-long relationship with GM. A variety of other businesses and entrepreneurs also thrived.

The city also survived a 100-year flood and implemented a flood prevention system that has kept the city flood-free ever since. And finally, Dayton
implemented and popularized a new form of municipal government that is
still in place today and has been widely copied. The ensuing decades would
see further growth in Dayton, but over the next 30 years Dayton would also
begin to lose some of its momentum.

CHAPTER 3

Dayton from 1930 to 1960

THE BEGINNING OF DECLINE

THE EARLY twentieth century was a period of innovation, institutional reform, and economic growth for Dayton. By 1930, however, things began to change, though many of the changes are more apparent to the modern onlooker than they were to the people of the day.

One of the most significant economic events in US history occurred during this period: the Great Depression. The Great Depression was an especially large and long-lasting recession, which is a contraction in economic output. In America, the National Bureau of Economic Research dates business cycles, and it defines a recession as "a significant decline in economic activity spread across the economy, lasting more than a few months."[1] The decline in economic activity that constituted the Great Depression occurred from August 1929 to March 1933, a period of 43 months. As a comparison, the recession that accompanied the housing bust and financial crisis in 2007 lasted only 18 months.

The Great Depression was a complicated event, and the exact causes are still being debated among economists and historians. That said, several factors that contributed to it have been identified. One argument is that a technology shock, making the economy less productive overall, could have

---

1. National Bureau of Economic Research, "US Business Cycle Expansions and Contractions," accessed December 4, 2017, http://www.nber.org/cycles.html.

caused the recession that eventually turned into the Depression, though the exact nature of this shock is unclear.[2] Many economists, such as Nobel Laureate Milton Friedman and former chair of the Federal Reserve Ben Bernanke, place much of the blame on monetary policy administered by the Federal Reserve, which involves controlling the supply of money in the economy. Specifically, they cite an adherence to the gold standard along with Federal Reserve actions that decreased the money supply and allowed banks to fail. These actions decreased liquidity, which slowed growth.[3] Still others point to the uncertainty generated by the stock market crash of 1929 and its negative effect on subsequent consumer spending.[4]

Regardless of the primary cause, from 1929 to 1933 US economic output fell by more than 38%, business investment fell nearly 80%, and household spending on consumer durables—such as cars and appliances—fell by more than 55%.[5] Over the same period, the unemployment rate increased from 3% to over 20%.[6] Even after the Great Recession of 2007–9, the Great Depression remains the largest and longest economic contraction since the 1870s. Factors that are associated with the especially long duration of the Great Depression and the slow recovery include sticky wages and policies that encouraged monopoly behavior by firms.

Sticky wages is a term used to describe the slow adjustment of wages relative to prices. When prices fall faster than wages, workers become expensive compared to the products firms are selling, and this leads to layoffs as firms try to keep costs under control. Wages can be sticky for a variety of reasons, including long-term contracts that specify wages and raises (common in contracts with labor unions), laws that prevent wages from falling below a certain level (e.g., the minimum wage), and concerns that wage cuts will hurt worker morale or reduce effort.[7] If wages weren't sticky and thus fell when revenue fell, there would be less need for layoffs during economic downturns.

---

2. Harold L. Cole and Lee E. Ohanian, "The Great Depression in the United States from a Neoclassical Perspective," *Handbook of Monetary and Fiscal Policy* (2001): 159.

3. Ben S. Bernanke, *The Macroeconomics of the Great Depression: A Comparative Approach, Journal of Money, Credit, and Banking* 27, no. 1 (1995): 1–28.

4. Christina D. Romer, "The Great Crash and the Onset of the Great Depression," *Quarterly Journal of Economics* 105, no. 3 (1990): 597–624.

5. Cole and Ohanian, "The Great Depression."

6. Robert A. Margo, "Employment and Unemployment in the 1930s," *Journal of Economic Perspectives* 7, no. 2 (1993): 41–59.

7. Carl M. Campbell III and Kunal S. Kamlani, "The Reasons for Wage Rigidity: Evidence from a Survey of Firms," *Quarterly Journal of Economics* 112, no. 3 (1997): 759–89.

The Great Depression was the catalyst for the New Deal, the largest peacetime expansion of federal government spending in US history.[8] Economists have identified several New Deal policies that likely contributed to sticky wages, including work relief policies—which forced private-sector employers to offer higher wages to entice workers off the relief rolls— government pressure on industry leaders to maintain high wages, and National Recovery Administration policies that encouraged fewer working hours per worker in combination with more workers and higher wages.[9]

Other researchers stress the role New Deal policies played in increasing monopoly power as a primary reason for the slow recovery in employment and output.[10] They argue that the suspension of antitrust law contained in the National Industrial Recovery Act of 1933 encouraged firms to collaborate on price and output decisions, with the result being higher prices and less output. Moreover, in return for the government-sanctioned collusion that allowed firms to raise their prices, firms helped the Roosevelt administration achieve its goal of higher wages by giving raises to current workers.

In addition to the policies designed to prop up wages, the New Deal also included several grant programs with various goals. About half of the New Deal grants went to relief programs for the poor and unemployed; another 20% of the grants went to World War I veterans, including a cash bonus; and 18% of the grants funded large public works projects, such as a series of dams along the Tennessee River that also gave rise to the government-sponsored Tennessee Valley Authority (TVA). Interestingly, the first chairman of the TVA was none other than Arthur Morgan, the principal design engineer for the Miami Conservancy District's flood protection system that protects Dayton to this day. Finally, the final 12% of New Deal grants was given to farmers, including payments to keep land out of production in order to decrease the supply and raise the prices of agricultural products.[11]

The overall success of these programs is mixed.[12] The public works and relief spending didn't have much of an effect on total income or private-sector employment, though it did help lower mortality and crime rates. The farm grants aided large farmers but hurt smaller ones. The outcomes of the other grant programs were similarly mixed. Further evidence for the

8. Price V. Fishback, "How Successful Was the New Deal? The Microeconomic Impact of New Deal Spending and Lending Policies in the 1930s" (Working Paper No. 21925, National Bureau of Economic Research, 2016).

9. Fishback, "How Successful Was the New Deal?," 28.

10. Cole and Ohanian, "The Great Depression," 10.

11. Fishback, "How Successful Was the New Deal?," 7.

12. Fishback, "How Successful Was the New Deal?," 27.

mixed overall success of New Deal policies is that by 1939, ten years after the Depression first began and several years after most of the New Deal policies were implemented, the economy had yet to recover: Economic output was still 29% lower in 1939 than it was in 1929.

The Great Depression had a significant effect on nearly every part of America, and Dayton was no exception. Large declines in output led to layoffs and high rates of unemployment. For example, the workforce of NCR, the city's largest employer, fell by 59%—from 8,500 to 3,500—from 1930 to 1933.[13] Without jobs, people struggled to make ends meet and pay their property taxes, and Dayton's tax revenue declined accordingly. In 1933 Dayton's delinquent taxes totaled $3.1 million, and this increased to $8.7 million in 1935.[14] Adjusted for inflation, those amounts are equal to approximately $57 million and $150 million respectively, which are significant sums. In fact, $150 million would have made up over 40% of Dayton's total revenues in 2015. Such a large decline would strain any city's finances.

According to one account, the decline in tax revenue caused liquidity problems, and as early as 1930 Dayton was paying city workers in scrip that it promised to redeem later for cash. The scrip was also accepted by businesses in the Dayton area in lieu of cash since the businesses could use it as payment for city or county taxes or other city fees.[15] Nearly 10,000 city residents had applied for relief by 1931, and in 1932 Dayton's budget was stretched so thin that it removed lightbulbs from city-owned lights to save money on electricity costs. That same year, voters passed a one-half mil property tax levy and the proceeds were used to provide aid to the expanding poor population, some of whom took city jobs that paid $3.60 per day in food vouchers. Private organizations chipped in as well: The NCR women's club ran a soup kitchen, and the city's movie theaters allowed customers to pay in canned goods, which were distributed to the poor and jobless.

Like other large cities in America, Dayton received some of the New Deal grants, including Works Progress Administration (WPA) grants for infrastructure projects. The WPA was one of the programs intended to provide poverty relief by hiring the unemployed to work on public projects. It was created in 1935, and at its peak in 1938 it employed over three million people.

---

13. Tom Dunham, *Dayton in the 20th Century* (self-pub., AuthorHouse, 2005), 78.

14. Dunham, *Dayton*, 78.

15. Loren Gatch, "Tax Anticipation Scrip as a Form of Local Currency in the USA during the 1930s," *International Journal of Community Currency Research* 16 (2012): D22–35; Dayton, Ohio, Tax Anticipation Notes, http://depressionscrip.com/ohio/ohio.html.

As to the WPA's general effect, economists Todd Neumann, Price Fish-back, and Shawn Kantor find that WPA grants increased monthly earnings in cities that received them but had a negative effect on private-sector employment.[16] As mentioned earlier, by providing some income and stability during a time of economic uncertainty, work-relief programs increased the wages private sector employers had to pay to entice people off relief roles. As a result, employers hired fewer people. The authors suggest this is why the WPA had a negative effect on private employment. Thus, by crowding out some private-sector jobs, the WPA contributed to the slow recovery of Dayton's private sector during the Depression.

Though the WPA slowed the overall recovery, it helped Dayton with several projects that should be familiar to Dayton residents today. In 1937 WPA grants helped Dayton pave three runways, build two hangars, and install a lighting system for its recently acquired airport. Fifteen years later the airport would officially be named the James M. Cox Dayton Municipal Airport, after the Ohio governor and *Dayton Daily News* founder who oversaw its purchase. WPA funds were also used to complete the transformation of the Dayton portion of the Miami and Erie Canal into Patterson Boulevard. The canal had sat unused since the early 1900s—a stinking, garbage-filled eyesore—until the completion of the boulevard in 1939.

Despite the positive effect of the WPA grants on Dayton's infrastructure, Dayton's economy was still weak during the late 1930s. One measure of an area's economic vitality is retail sales per person, and it was not until 1939 that sales returned to 1929 levels in Montgomery County.[17] In other Ohio counties such as Lucas, Hamilton, and adjacent Greene County—whose county seats are Toledo, Cincinnati, and Xenia, respectively—retail sales per person were still below their 1929 levels in 1939. Dayton, along with the rest of the country, did not experience a robust recovery in economic output until the country ramped up manufacturing production due to World War II.

Once the United States entered the war, private-sector construction and manufacturing declined considerably as the country's resources were allocated to war production. Programs like the WPA, which was terminated in 1943, no longer provided steady jobs, but it didn't matter since the demand caused by the war was an economic boon to manufacturing cities like Day-

---

16. Todd C. Neumann, Price V. Fishback, and Shawn Kantor, "The Dynamics of Relief Spending and the Private Urban Labor Market during the New Deal," *Journal of Economic History* 70, no. 1 (2010): 195–220.

17. Price Fishback, "New Deal Data: Data Set for Geographic Distribution of New Deal Spending by Counties," University of Arizona, accessed January 31, 2019, http://www.u.arizona.edu/~fishback/Published_Research_Datasets.html.

ton. Major Dayton companies such as NCR, Delco, Frigidaire, and others secured government contracts totaling over $1.5 billion. NCR manufactured bomb fuses, rocket motors, and decrypting machines; Frigidaire manufactured Browning machine guns; and Delco manufactured a variety of products, including bomber landing gear assemblies, diesel generators for watercraft, and 37 mm shells.[18]

All these government contracts required workers, and by 1943 total city employment was 124% higher than it had been in 1933. NCR's employment surpassed its predepression level of 8,500 and reached 20,000 during the war, and over 37,000 civilians were employed at nearby Wright Field (today Wright-Patterson Air Force Base) during the peak years of the war.[19] The employment boom was also reflected in the area's population growth. Dayton's population grew from 210,000 to 243,000 during the 1940s, while Montgomery County's population increased from 295,000 to 398,000. Thus about 70% of the county's growth in the 1940s occurred in cities and towns other than Dayton, which is reflective of the widespread suburbanization that was occurring throughout the country. In previous decades, Dayton accounted for nearly all of Montgomery County's population growth. The trend of faster county growth outside of Dayton continued through the 1960s and ultimately weakened Dayton's position as the area's economic center.

However, Dayton's decline relative to the surrounding suburban cities would not be fully recognized for several more years, and Dayton's strategic location was still lauded into the 1950s. In 1959 the northeast quadrant of the United States—of which Dayton is a part—contained 46% of the national population, 52% of its income, and 65% of its manufacturing activity. The center for consumer markets was approximately 250 miles west of Dayton, and the center of industrial markets was approximately 150 miles to the northeast of the city. The authors of a comprehensive study of Dayton and Montgomery County completed in 1959 concluded, "Clearly, Metropolitan Dayton is in a very good general location."[20]

Despite this optimism, someone familiar with Dayton's history could already see the population trends working against it. In 1926 the center of the country's urban population was 34 miles from Dayton, while the median

---

18. "NCR Corporation History," Funding Universe, accessed January 31, 2019, http://www.fundinguniverse.com/company-histories/ncr-corporation-history/; David D. Jackson, "The American Automobile Industry in World War Two," accessed June 25, 2018, http://usautoindustryworldwartwo.com/generalmotors.htm.

19. Dunham, *Dayton*, 81.

20. Metropolitan Community Studies, *Metropolitan Challenge: Study of the People, the Government, and the Economy of Metropolitan Dayton* (Dayton, 1959), 171 (hereafter cited as *Metropolitan Challenge*).

point of the total population was 43 miles away. Yet by 1959 the center of the consumer population was approximately 250 miles west. Even though these numbers do not measure the same thing, it's clear that the locational advantage of Dayton was diminishing.

Dayton's population continued to increase through the 1930s, '40s, and '50s, as shown in figure 1, though at a slower pace. But contrary to the optimistic projections of the 1920s, it never hit 400,000 or even 300,000.[21] By the 1960s Dayton's population was declining from its peak of 262,332 people, and many other midwestern and northeastern cities were following the same path.

Though it might seem shocking today, the problems that occupied the minds of many local politicians and city planners in the 1950s were related to growth rather than decline. Referring to the 180 metropolitan regions in the United States in 1959, researchers studying the Dayton area said:

> Most of them are experiencing the pains of rapid development; few have escaped the difficulties that accompany growth. . . . A large number of the same questions are heard, whether one is in New York, Denver, or Metropolitan Dayton.[22]

According to these researchers, "the difficulties that accompany growth" include congestion, urban blight and "haphazard" growth, which they define as growth that does not proceed according to some sort of regional plan. Local populations and their political leaders appear to have always preferred stable populations to growing or shrinking ones. In a survey conducted by the same researchers, 50% of Dayton area residents thought that the current (late 1950s) population was "about right" and an additional 20% thought it was already too large. Only 30% wanted the population to continue growing.

It is understandable that many people prefer stability. Stability is relatively easy to manage in the present and easy to plan for—it's certain and safe. Growth brings change, not all of which is beneficial to all people, and

---

21. The idea of a metropolitan area as a collection of separate yet economically related municipalities was not well formed in the 1920s. Thus, the 1920s projections could be interpreted as relating to an area like the modern Dayton metropolitan area rather than the political city of Dayton. That said, it's not clear how large the area the authors may have had in mind would have been, since modern metropolitan areas are delineated based on commuting patterns, which were likely very different in the 1920s when cars were still relatively new and roads were of poorer quality.

22. *Metropolitan Challenge*, 87.

the uncertainty as to whether one will benefit from growth or be harmed by it causes many to oppose it.

Unfortunately, the labor market equilibrium required for urban populations to stabilize in the long run doesn't exist. Both the entrepreneurial process and technological change are constantly altering relative wages across areas and the value of place-specific amenities. These changes induce people to migrate to new locations, which leads to further migration, and so on. Even if a temporary equilibrium is reached, it is only a matter of time before some aspiring entrepreneur invents something that starts the process all over again. Keeping this process in mind makes it clear that cities are largely faced with the alternatives of growing or shrinking.

Contrary to the residents' fear of further growth, the city of Dayton began to decline in regional importance during this period. In 1930, 73% of Montgomery County's population resided in Dayton. By 1940 it had declined slightly to 71%. However, after 1940 the decline accelerated dramatically: in 1950 only 61% of the county's population lived in Dayton, and by 1958 the percentage had further declined to only 53%.[23] This relative population decline occurred despite a 43% increase in the geographic size of the city of Dayton from 1930 to 1960, due largely to annexation. The total land area of Dayton in 1930 was 18.1 square miles, and it increased to 23.7 square miles in 1940 and 33.6 square miles in 1960.[24]

The migration of young parents with children from the city to the suburbs was obvious by 1958. In that year 69% of the suburban residents of Montgomery County were less than 35 years old, compared to only 55% in the city of Dayton and 60% in the rural, outer zone.[25] Of these three areas, the suburban area also had the highest proportion of professional workers, proprietors, and managers—what labor economists today would label high-skill workers. Thirty-two percent of working suburban residents were employed in the high-skill occupations, compared to 23% in Dayton. Service workers and laborers were more concentrated in the city—14% versus only 8% in the suburban zone.

---

23. *Metropolitan Challenge.*

24. "Table 16: Population of the 100 Largest Urban Places: 1930," US Census Bureau, June 15, 1998, http://www.census.gov/population/www/documentation/twps0027/tab16.txt;"Table 17: Population of the 100 Largest Urban Places: 1940," US Census Bureau, June 15, 1998, http://www.census.gov/population/www/documentation/twps0027/tab17.txt.

25. The suburban zone in 1958 consisted of the local governmental units located in the urban area bordering the city of Dayton. It included the townships of Harrison, Mad River, Madison, and Van Buren as well as Oakwood, Riverside, Trotwood, Kettering, and Moraine (*Metropolitan Challenge*, 9).

The migration of educated residents from the city had also become evident by 1958. In Dayton, only 8% of adults were college graduates, compared to 17% in the suburban zone. Table 1 shows the breakdown of educational attainment by area in 1958.

TABLE 1. Dayton area educational attainment, 1958. (Data from *Metropolitan Challenge*, 20.)

LEVEL OF EDUCATION	DAYTON	SUBURBAN	OUTER	TOTAL
8th grade or less	23%	21%	18%	21%
Some high school	26	15	25	23
High school graduate	35	39	43	39
Some college	7	7	11	8
College graduate	8	17	3	10

The educational attainment of an area's labor force at a given time is a strong predictor of subsequent population growth. Dayton's relatively uneducated labor force in 1958 was certainly a factor in its decline in the latter part of the twentieth century. We will discuss the relationship between education and city growth more in chapter 4.

As mentioned earlier, Dayton's land area grew by over 15 square miles from 1930 to 1960, largely via annexation of neighboring communities, but in hindsight this was likely a mistake since more land area has costs as well as benefits. In this period of regional prosperity, Dayton officials likely believed that annexing nearby communities would allow them to capture the tax revenue of the more affluent suburban areas that were forming as people migrated out of the city center. But after 1960, when even these more suburban neighborhoods began to lose population, this additional land became relatively costly since city infrastructure had to be maintained over a wider, less dense area. From 1930 to 1960, Dayton's population density declined from over 11,000 people per square mile to approximately 7,800 people per square mile. By 2000 the city's population density had fallen below 3,000 people per square mile.

There is evidence that per capita infrastructure expenditures on highways and sewer systems decline as population density increases in cities under 500,000 people, implying that the decline in Dayton's population density over time raised such expenditures.[26] Yet on average there appears to be

---

26. Randall G. Holcombe and DeEdgra W. Williams, "The Impact of Population Density on Municipal Government Expenditures," *Public Finance Review* 36, no. 3 (2008): 359–73.

little effect on total per capita expenditures due to the countervailing effect density has on the cost of police and fire services. However, later we will see that the cost of government services in Dayton increased during the latter half of the twentieth century as population density was declining.

Manufacturing in Decline

The decline of manufacturing employment in America is often viewed as a cause of the Midwest's economic decline. Many midwestern cities, including Dayton, were manufacturing hubs and the composition of the local economies reflected that: In 1945 manufacturing employment was 55% of total employment in the Dayton area. But from 1945 to 1958, manufacturing employment in the Dayton area only increased by 14%, compared to 23% for employment in general. As a result, by 1958 manufacturing had fallen from 55% of the Dayton area's total employment to 46% of total employment. Even then, experts recognized that the decline of manufacturing employment was likely to continue.[27] More machinery in manufacturing had already automated many tasks formerly completed manually, and the keen observer could see that this was unlikely to end.

The decline of manufacturing employment in the years after World War II was not unique to Dayton and Montgomery County. Similar declines from 1947 to 1957 in the proportion of manufacturing employment occurred in other Ohio counties, including Summit (67.6% to 58.3%), Stark (67.6% to 62.3%), Cuyahoga (55% to 50.7%), and Lucas (56.4% to 47.2%) as well as Ohio as a whole (57.1% to 52.8%).[28]

Alternatively, Hamilton County (51.3% to 50.5%) and Franklin County (40.6% to 40.5%) were less affected.[29] As we will discuss later, it's not a coincidence that Cincinnati and Columbus, located in Hamilton County and Franklin County respectively, are the two large Ohio cities best adapting to the modern service and knowledge economy. Their economies, particularly Columbus's, relied less on manufacturing from the start, which made the adjustment to a service economy less painful.

Manufacturing employment had begun its move to lower cost regions of the country by the 1950s. The percentage of total payrolls in manufacturing in the Great Lakes region fell from 47.4% in 1947 to 45.7% in 1957.

---

27. *Metropolitan Challenge*, 28.

28. These counties are the homes of major Ohio cities Akron, Canton, Cleveland, and Toledo, respectively.

29. These counties are the homes of major Ohio cities Cincinnati and Columbus.

The New England region experienced an even larger drop, from 46.9% to 41.9%. Meanwhile, the proportion of payrolls in manufacturing rose in the Southwest (16% to 19.1%), Plains (25.8% to 27.7%), Rocky Mountain (14.7% to 16.1%), and Pacific West (22.8% to 28.5%) regions over the same 10-year period.

Despite this relative decline, manufacturing was still the primary sector of the Dayton metro area's economy throughout the decade. In 1957 manufacturing workers earned $600 million in total income and the sector still employed nearly half of the labor force. Capital investments had increased the productivity of workers, so total income was rising even though the level of employment wasn't. As a comparison, workers in the small but growing finance, insurance, and real estate sectors only earned $30 million in total income in the same year.

The relative decline of manufacturing employment from 1945 to 1958 may have hurt some manufacturing workers, but in terms of income the Dayton metro area's economy did well over this period. Total real income in the Dayton metro area—which at this time included all of Montgomery County—as measured by payrolls increased by 50%, and average real total earnings increased by 20%.[30] On a per capita basis the region was performing well relative to the state: In Montgomery County per capita income in 1957 was $2,600 compared to $2,255 in the state of Ohio and $2,027 in the nation as a whole.[31] Unfortunately for the people of Dayton, these high earnings wouldn't last. As we will see later, the increase in earnings during this period contrasts with the steady fall of relative average wages that the Dayton metro area experienced after 1969 and that the city has experienced more recently.

Segregation in Dayton

Though Dayton's economy generally did well in the decades immediately after World War II, the city still had its problems. The middle part of the twentieth century was a time of intense racial segregation throughout the United States, and Dayton was a highly segregated city. A 1988 study found that the housing patterns in Dayton and its suburbs in 1980 were the third most racially segregated out of the 50 largest US metro areas, behind only

---

30. *Metropolitan Challenge.*
31. *Metropolitan Challenge.*

Chicago and Cleveland.[32] This result has its roots in federal policies and black rural-to-urban migration that began in the 1910s and continued until the 1970s.

In 1910 only 3% of Dayton's population was black.[33] Fifty years later, over 20% of the population was black. This influx of blacks, primarily from the South, was not unique to Dayton. The migration of blacks—and southern whites—to the North accelerated after 1915 due to an increase in demand for factory and manual labor because of World War I, a decline in European immigration, and bad harvests in the South due to the spread of the boll weevil, a beetle that feeds on cotton buds. The bad harvests decreased demand for southern agricultural workers, which lowered wages, while wages in the North increased due to the wartime demand. Average wages in the North had actually been higher than those in the South for some time, but it took a confluence of all of these events to drastically increase southern-to-northern migration. Black migration from the South to the North and West accelerated in the 1920s, declined in the 1930s during the Depression, and then shot up again in the 1940s. It remained relatively high until the 1970s, but by the 1980s more blacks were moving to the South than leaving it.[34]

Prior to World War I, many of the low-skill positions in northern urban factories and other businesses were filled by European immigrants, which delayed the migration of blacks to the North.[35] But the war disrupted transatlantic shipping routes, causing immigration to decline from over 1 million entrants annually to around 100,000. The federal government also implemented strict immigration quotas in the 1920s to curb immigration from Asia and eastern and southern Europe. The decline in immigration caused by World War I and the quotas meant northern businesses needed other sources of labor and some began to actively recruit in the South.

Blacks who migrated to the North post–World War I tended to be either low-skill manual laborers or relatively high-skill workers.[36] The higher wages attracted low-skill blacks and whites, while the better social and political

32. Douglas S. Massey and Nancy A. Denton, "Suburbanization and Segregation in US Metropolitan Areas," *American Journal of Sociology* 94, no. 3 (November 1988): 592–626.

33. 1910 Decennial Census data from 1% IPUMS sample. Steven Ruggles, Sarah Flood, Ronald Goeken, Josiah Grover, Erin Meyer, Jose Pacas, and Matthew Sobek. IPUMS USA: Version 8.0 [dataset]. Minneapolis, MN: IPUMS, 2018, https://doi.org/10.18128/D010.V8.0.

34. Leah Platt Boustan, *Competition in the Promised Land: Black Migrants in Northern Cities and Labor Markets* (Princeton, NJ: Princeton University Press, 2016), 22.

35. William J. Collins, "When the Tide Turned: Immigration and the Delay of the Great Black Migration," *Journal of Economic History* 57, no. 3 (1997): 607–32.

36. Boustan, *Competition*, 40.

climate available for blacks in the North was likely a contributing factor for the migration of high-skill blacks, especially since they experienced smaller financial gains from northern migration than low-skill blacks. Economist Leah Boustan estimates that northern migration resulted in roughly a 130% increase in earnings for blacks and a 60% increase in earnings for southern whites. Even after accounting for the higher cost of living in the North, she estimates that migration resulted in a 56% increase in real earnings for blacks and a 25% increase for whites on average.[37]

In Dayton, the blacks who moved northward in pursuit of higher wages and a better life clustered on the west side of the city. By 1960 Dayton was home to approximately 60,000 blacks and nearly all of them lived west of the Great Miami River, which served as the de facto boundary between the white and black portions of the city.

While it's tempting to attribute black-white segregation to racial animosity, it's also important to note that it can happen unintentionally. In his seminal work on segregation, Noble Prize–winning economist Thomas Schelling showed how individuals can become segregated by easily recognized characteristics, such as skin color, even if no one intentionally plans or desires such segregation.[38] In fact, even if both blacks and whites prefer to be around some people who have a different skin color, complete segregation can occur if people dislike being a minority within an area. For example, if everyone wants to live in a neighborhood where at least 51% of their neighbors look like them, there will be a high level of segregation since no one is willing to be a minority.

However, while extreme segregation can occur spontaneously, in Dayton it had some help from the federal government, particularly the Federal Housing Authority (FHA). Dayton home builders and owners often put restrictive covenants in their deeds forbidding the sale of the home to a black person, and from 1934 until 1950 such covenants were required if they wanted the FHA to insure the mortgages against losses due to defaults.[39] This was done to protect the FHA from a decline in home values that may have resulted from racially integrated neighborhoods. The only homes that did not have covenants were located on the west side of the Great Miami River.[40] Thus, blacks migrating from the South were more or less required

37. Boustan, *Competition*, 52–53.

38. Thomas C. Schelling, "Models of Segregation," *American Economic Review* 59, no. 2 (1969): 488–93.

39. Joseph Watras, "The Racial Desegregation of Dayton, Ohio, Public Schools, 1966–2008," *Ohio History* 117, no. 1 (2010): 93–107.

40. Watras, "Racial Desegregation."

to find housing on the west side of the city. Similar patterns of residential segregation existed in other northern cities in the mid-twentieth century: In 1940 the typical white resident of a northern city lived in a neighborhood that was 97% white.[41] As black migration to northern cities increased from 1940 to 1970, whites were typically able to maintain their separation by migrating to the largely white suburbs, leaving blacks living in the central city even more isolated from whites.

The segregation caused by the FHA policy was reinforced over time as additional blacks migrated to the west side, as explained by the analysis of the Great Black Migration by economists William Carrington, Enrica Detragiache, and Tara Vishwanath. They argue that the costs of northern migration declined as the number of similar migrants in the destination area increased.[42] One mechanism driving this result could be that previous migrants relayed valuable information about the destination's labor market to friends and family back home. There are also benefits to moving to areas where social networks have already been established, as this provides migrants with a network of family and friends upon arrival, easing the adjustment process.

By reducing the costs of future migration, the FHA policy that encouraged segregation also created a self-perpetuating mechanism that resulted in a large amount of racial segregation in Dayton by the mid-twentieth century. This racial segregation would impact Dayton in ways that were unanticipated in the early twentieth century when the policy was in place. We will discuss these consequences more when we analyze Dayton's population decline from the 1960s onward.

Signaling Dissatisfaction with Local Government: Vote or Leave?

As we discussed earlier, in the 1940s and 1950s people moving to the Dayton area began settling outside of Dayton's city limits in larger numbers. There's also some evidence that families with young children and more educated adults were leaving the city to live in the surrounding suburbs. One reason for these changing settlement patterns may have been a decline in the quality of government in Dayton compared to nearby municipalities.

---

41. Boustan, *Competition*, 97.

42. William J. Carrington, Enrica Detragiache, and Tara Vishwanath, "Migration with Endogenous Moving Costs," *American Economic Review* 86, no. 4 (September 1996): 909–30.

It's difficult to measure the quality of government goods and services since they are not sold in a market and thus lack accurate price signals and profit and loss signals. That said, one way to gauge the quality of government goods and services is from surveys of residents. Surveys are not perfect since what people say about a service can deviate from how much they actually value it relative to the available alternatives, but they do provide some relevant information. Surveys conducted in the late 1950s on resident dissatisfaction with local government services in Dayton and the surrounding area provide some information about Dayton residents' satisfaction with government compared to other area residents' satisfaction with their governments.[43]

According to these surveys, Dayton residents were generally less dissatisfied with their government than other residents in most of the surrounding areas. Residents from Oakwood—a small city on Dayton's southern border—expressed the lowest rates of dissatisfaction (15% were dissatisfied with one or more services), but Dayton residents expressed less dissatisfaction than neighboring Kettering residents and those of other nearby towns and municipalities. In Dayton 55% of residents were dissatisfied with one or more services, compared to 81% of Kettering's residents and 83% of all suburban residents.

However, the proportion of people who felt like complaining about local government services—and thus ostensibly were dissatisfied—but didn't complain was higher in Dayton than many of the surrounding areas. Thirty-two percent of Dayton's residents felt like complaining but didn't, compared to 25% of all residents in the suburban zone and 26% of all residents in the more rural outer zone. Meanwhile, the proportion of people who did complain was generally the same or lower in Dayton, especially when compared to other jurisdictions within the suburban zone—15% of the residents in Dayton actually complained to a public agency or official versus 22% of all suburban zone residents.

Additionally, of the proportion of residents who felt like complaining, the proportion who actually did was lower in Dayton than in other jurisdictions as a whole in the suburban zone (32% versus 47%) and lower than other municipalities in the outer zone (32% versus 38%). What this means is that relative to the surrounding municipalities, Dayton had a larger proportion of people who were dissatisfied with some aspect of their local government but didn't let officials know about it.

---

43. *Metropolitan Challenge*, 284.

Voter turnout in Dayton and surrounding cities was also low. An average of 42% of registered voters participated in local elections in Dayton from 1950 to 1958. For state and national elections, the average increased to 75%. This pattern held for the other municipalities in Montgomery County as well, such as Kettering (49% and 76%), Miamisburg (53% and 79%), Oakwood (55% and 79%), and Vandalia (61% and 78%). In each city, participation among registered voters in local elections was substantially lower than participation in state and national elections. That said, the voting gaps in these other municipalities were not as large as Dayton's.

There are three options available for voters who want government services to improve: (1) vote in an election to express dissatisfaction with the current local government, knowing that any one vote is unlikely to change the outcome; (2) complain or protest for change; and (3) migrate to a community that better matches their preferences for local government services. The costs are usually highest for option 3, but so are the benefits since the person will receive a direct increase in happiness and satisfaction from moving to the preferred location.

On the other hand, if a voter's preferred election outcome does not materialize, they get no benefit from voting. Moreover, there is the real possibility that the voter's preferred outcome is not even one of the choices. The efficacy of protesting is also uncertain since it depends on the credibility of the threat made by the protesters.

It's the difference between the costs and benefits of the options, or the net benefits, that determines whether residents vote at the ballot box, complain, or vote with their feet by moving. Since even in local elections the probability of any one vote swinging an election is small, individuals who are dissatisfied with their local government often conclude that voting with their feet rather than at the ballot box is a more effective way to get the government they want. The benefits of moving to the preferred location are obvious and the costs to move within the same state or metro area are relatively small compared to international migration. So even though voting with one's feet is more costly than traditional voting or complaining, it's also more beneficial, which makes it an attractive option for many people.

According to the surveys presented here, Dayton residents were less dissatisfied with government than many other nearby residents. However, Dayton residents were also less likely to vote or complain to signal dissatisfaction than residents of other areas. Since these are only two surveys from one point in time, we should be careful about inferring too much from them. That said, beginning in the 1960s many residents left Dayton, and some of this outmigration may have been a manifestation of the unexpressed discontent with local government revealed in these surveys.

The 1930s through the 1950s was a period of lows and highs for Dayton. The Great Depression put thousands out of work in the city and damaged the city's finances. But it also brought in federal government grants that filled in the Miami and Erie Canal and helped improve the city's airport. Still, it took the Dayton area about a decade to recover from the Depression.

America's entry into World War II was a boon for the city's manufacturing industry and companies like NCR and Delco hired thousands of additional workers. The city's population increased accordingly, growing from about 200,000 people in 1930 to over 262,000 by 1960, while the county's population grew from 273,000 to over 527,000. And due to greater productivity, at the end of the 1950s people in Montgomery County earned relatively high incomes compared to people in the rest of Ohio.

It was also during this period that racial segregation began to solidify itself in Dayton. Blacks, generally migrating from the South, clustered on the city's west side while whites largely remained in the east. The migration of blacks and southern whites to the North, along with the decline in US manufacturing employment, the construction of the interstate highway system, and rising crime, would affect Dayton in the decades to come.

Permission to reprint the following photos in the book has been granted by Dayton History and the release forms are available from author.

PHOTO 1. The Wright brothers (*left,* Orville; *right,* Wilbur) and their plane and hangar at Simms Station near Huffman Prairie in May 1904. Huffman Prairie, located just outside of Dayton, is where the Wright brothers mastered the art of flying.

PHOTO 2. Edward Deeds's barn, 319 Central Avenue, Dayton, circa 1910. It was here that Deeds, Charles Kettering, and the rest of the "Barn Gang" created the electric starter and several other automobile-related inventions.

PHOTO 3. The Delco building, 329 East First Street, during the 1913 flood. Today the building is named Delco Lofts and contains apartments.

PHOTO 4. Aerial view of Dayton in 1933. Today I-75 runs north-south through the middle of this scene and the neighborhoods to the west (*left*) of downtown and in the bottom-middle of this picture are no longer there, as can be seen in photo 8.

PHOTO 5. North side of West Third Street looking east in 1941. The Wright brothers' famous bicycle shop, 1127 West Third Street, stood where the used car lot is until it was removed by Henry Ford for his museum in 1936–37.

PHOTO 6. Aerial view of the NCR factory complex, March 4, 1948. The portion of circular track on the left side is part of the Montgomery County Fairgrounds. Today this area is mostly fields and parking lots.

PHOTO 7. Automobile starters being assembled on the production line at Delco. This photo shows how labor-intensive manufacturing once was.

PHOTO 8. Aerial view of Dayton and US Route 35 and I-75 interchange, mid-1990s. US 35 is under construction (*upper right*). In photo 4, there were neighborhoods where the interchange is and along the river, west of downtown (*top left*). Both neighborhoods were razed to make room for I-75.

PHOTO 9. Rike's Department Store at the corner of West Second Street (*left*) and Main Street. The store's white parking garage on Second Street (*far left*) is an example of downtown retailers adding parking to compete with suburban stores. Today the site is occupied by the Schuster Performing Arts Center.

PHOTO 10. Aerial view of Moraine Assembly, January 1985. Located in Moraine, Ohio, a suburb of Dayton, it was a Frigidaire appliance plant from 1951 to 1975. At the time of this photo, General Motors used the plant to assemble Chevrolet Blazers and GMC Jimmys. GM ceased operations here in 2008, and today part of the plant is occupied by Fuyao Glass, which makes glass products for the auto industry.

CHAPTER 4

Dayton from 1960 to 2010

DECLINE AND STAGNATION

THERE ARE four events that researchers and casual observers alike associate with the pervasive urban decline that took place in the Midwest and Northeast in the last half of twentieth century: (1) white flight, (2) construction of the interstate highway system, (3) the decline of US manufacturing employment, and (4) higher crime rates. Economists have found evidence that each of these factors played a role in the decline of cities, and in this chapter, we'll see how these findings explain the decline of Dayton in particular and other Rust Belt cities more generally.

Southern Migration and White Flight

As mentioned previously, Dayton became a racially segregated city in the late twentieth century. It also has a rather turbulent racial history. For example, in 1966 a riot erupted in Dayton after Lester Mitchell, who was black, was murdered by a group of white men while sweeping the sidewalk in front of his apartment. Ohio governor James Rhodes eventually sent 1,000 national guardsmen to Dayton to help control the situation.[1] One person was

---

1. Walter C. Rucker and James N. Upton, eds. *Encyclopedia of American Race Riots*, vol. 2 (Westport, CT: Greenwood Publishing Group, 2007), 148.

killed and 130 people were arrested during the riot. Such riots occurred in other industrial cities around the same time, with perhaps the most famous occurring in Detroit in 1967, and they exemplify the racial tension that existed in cities across America.

In 1979 the US Supreme Court approved a citywide busing plan for Dayton meant to desegregate the city's public schools.[2] The case was initiated in 1972 but the busing did not start until 1976 and was kept in place during the appeals process from 1976 until its ultimate approval in 1979. The system remained in place until 2002, at which time a federal judge dissolved the order.[3]

Events such as riots and government-mandated busing plans are often associated with the decline of central cities in the late twentieth century as a part of so-called "white flight." Economist Leah Boustan finds evidence supporting the traditional story of post–World War II white flight from the central cities to the suburbs.[4] She estimates that each black arrival in a northern city between 1940 and 1970 led to 2.7 white departures on average. The finding of more than one white departure for every black arrival suggests that race may have played a role in whites leaving cities. However, because poverty and race are highly correlated, Boustan notes it is difficult to distinguish whether the outflow of whites was primarily due to a distaste for race or a distaste for the lower incomes of southern arrivals.

In addition to race and income factors, another potential explanation for white departures is that the south-to-north migration caused local policies to change due to changes in the electorate. In other words, southern migrants wanted different government policies than northern residents, which caused northern city residents—who were generally white—to move to the suburbs to maintain their preferred fiscal policies and other public policies.[5]

Regarding this policy explanation, the evidence points to a distaste for lower incomes as the driver of white flight, not racial animus. As discussed previously, many southern migrants—both black and white—moved north in the pursuit of higher wages, meaning they tended to be relatively poor upon arrival. As a result, some northern whites left the city for the suburbs

---

2. Thomas Flygare, "Dayton II: School Desegregation on a Roller Coaster," Phi Delta Kappan 61, no. 2 (1979): 124–25.

3. James Hannah, "Judge Ends Racial Busing in Dayton," Cincinnati Enquirer, April 16, 2002.

4. Leah P. Boustan, "Was Postwar Suburbanization 'White Flight'? Evidence from the Black Migration," Quarterly Journal of Economics 125, no. 1 (2010): 417–43.

5. Leah Platt Boustan, Competition in the Promised Land: Black Migrants in Northern Cities and Labor Markets (Princeton, NJ: Princeton University Press, 2016), 130.

to avoid the social problems (e.g., more crime and lower quality schools) that typically arise in places with low average incomes and high poverty rates. An analysis of housing price differences on the border between city neighborhoods and neighboring suburbs using data from 1960 to 1980 finds that the share of blacks in a municipality had no effect on housing price differences once each area's median income is considered.[6] Lower median incomes, on the other hand, were associated with lower city housing values along the city–suburb border. This is consistent with northern city residents having a distaste for the lower incomes of southern migrants, which manifested as lower housing values in areas with a lot of recent migrants.

The higher housing prices in the primarily white, suburban neighborhoods were also associated with lower property tax rates, lower expenditures on police for a similar amount of safety, and a larger share of college-educated residents, which is considered a proxy for overall student quality in the local schools.[7] People are attracted to areas with higher-quality schools because students at these schools require fewer tax dollars to achieve a given level of academic proficiency.

In general, it doesn't appear that higher-income whites moved to the suburbs to avoid blacks per se, but rather to avoid the social problems often associated with low incomes, such as crime and lower school quality, and to avoid the higher taxes often levied to deal with such problems. However, this general finding shouldn't be construed as a claim that racism didn't exist and didn't contribute to some people's decisions to leave cities. Instead, to the extent that racism was a motivating factor, it was often accompanied by other concerns.

Yet it's important to recognize that white flight due to a distaste for black neighbors or lower incomes is in no small part due to the institution of chattel slavery. Slavery's role in any racial motivation for white flight is obvious, but slavery also contributed to lower incomes in the South for both blacks and less-educated whites. The desire to maintain slavery and its associated agricultural economy contributed to the lack of industrialization in the South relative to the North during the nineteenth century, and less industrialization resulted in lower average wages for all southern workers.[8] In this way, slavery also contributed to the economic conditions that made migration to the North financially attractive.

----

6. Boustan, *Competition*, 138.

7. Leah Platt Boustan, "Local Public Goods and the Demand for High-Income Municipalities," *Journal of Urban Economics* 76 (2013): 71–82.

8. David R. Meyer, "The Industrial Retardation of Southern Cities, 1860–1880," *Explorations in Economic History* 25, no. 4 (1988): 366–86.

Another study by economist William Frey examines metro area data from 1965 to 1970 and finds little evidence that traditional racial factors affected the decision of whites to move. However, he does find that the percentage of blacks in the city affected the location choice of whites once they decided to move: A higher proportion of blacks in the central city made it more likely that whites chose a suburban location. Frey does not find any effect from mandated school desegregation or riots on white flight.[9] In general, he largely attributes white migration to the suburbs to the relocation of employment opportunities and deteriorating economic conditions within the city.

On the other hand, Boustan uses data from the 1970s and finds that government-mandated school desegregation resulted in a decrease in demand for central city housing in affected metro areas.[10] The decrease in demand then caused housing prices to fall and eroded the city's tax base. Boustan attributes the fall in housing demand that accompanied mandated school desegregation to residents' concerns about changes in the racial composition of schools and the forced reassignment of children to schools outside of their neighborhood, such as what occurred in Dayton until 2002.

Anecdotally, my parents decided to move out of Dayton in the late 1980s when they unexpectedly received notice that I was to be bused from the east side of the city to the west side. I was in elementary school at the time, and my parents were concerned about the longer bus ride, which was approximately one hour versus the 15- or 20-minute ride I would have had if I attended my neighborhood school. Additionally, cross-city busing was assigned randomly from the resident's perspective, and my parents didn't appreciate the city suddenly changing where their child would attend school. Having no say in the matter was an important contributor to my parents' decision to leave Dayton, and I suspect many other parents who left Dayton due to busing felt similarly.

Though the evidence for the traditional story of white flight due to widespread racial prejudice is inconclusive, there is a preponderance of evidence that southern migration, whether due to racial factors or income factors, affected the likelihood that northern whites migrated to the suburbs. In this

9. William H. Frey, "Central City White Flight: Racial and Nonracial Causes," *American Sociological Review* 44, no. 3 (June 1979): 425–48. Frey's school desegregation data only include desegregation actions that occurred prior to 1970, which does not include Dayton's event. He acknowledges that the desegregation actions likely to elicit the largest effect did not occur until 1971 and beyond; thus, this result should be interpreted with caution when applied to Dayton.

10. Leah Platt Boustan, "School Desegregation and Urban Change: Evidence from City Boundaries," *American Economic Journal: Applied Economics* 4, no. 1 (2012): 85–108.

way, the influx of poorer southern blacks in the mid-twentieth century—and to a lesser extent poorer southern whites—explains some of the subsequent decline in Dayton's population of higher-income, educated whites along with its overall population. That said, the underlying cause of this effect is America's unfortunate history of chattel slavery that fostered racial animosity and prevented the South from industrializing.

The effects of southern migration on Dayton's population can be seen in figure 3. Dayton's black population increased dramatically from 1940 to 1970: during that period, nearly 54,000 blacks migrated to Dayton. Meanwhile, approximately 41,000 whites left Dayton from 1950 to 1970. These data are consistent with Boustan's research findings.[11]

In fact, nearly all of Dayton's overall population decline from 1960 to 1990 was due to the decline in the white population. As a result, the percentage of the population that was black steadily increased, from 10% in 1940, then 30% in 1970, and finally to 40% in 1990, which is near where it remains today.

The Interstate Highway System, Housing Policies, and Suburbanization

The evolution of US transportation infrastructure also contributed to Dayton's decline. The idea of an interstate highway system was developed in the 1930s and 1940s by various state and federal planning agencies and committees.[12] The automobile was ubiquitous by this time and urban congestion was becoming a significant problem. Many highway supporters also believed that highways were needed to *reverse* urban decay more generally. Unfortunately for cities like Dayton, those supporters got it backwards.

In Montgomery County, auto registrations increased from 36,381 in 1923 to 67,058 in 1929, and the congestion that came with them contributed to Dayton's decision to create a planning board made up of seven citizens serv-

---

11. Boustan's finding of 2.7 white departures per black arrival is from a multivariable regression that holds other factors constant; readers should thus be careful when comparing it to the unconditional effect in Dayton, which is 0.6 white departures per black arrival from 1940 to 1970. On the surface, the effect of a black arrival looks smaller in Dayton, but if other factors that affect white departures were accounted for, such as declining employment opportunities, the isolated effect of a black arrival in Dayton might be the same or larger than Boustan's finding.

12. Cliff Ellis, "Interstate Highways, Regional Planning and the Reshaping of Metropolitan America," *Planning Practice and Research* 16, no. 3-4 (2001): 247–69.

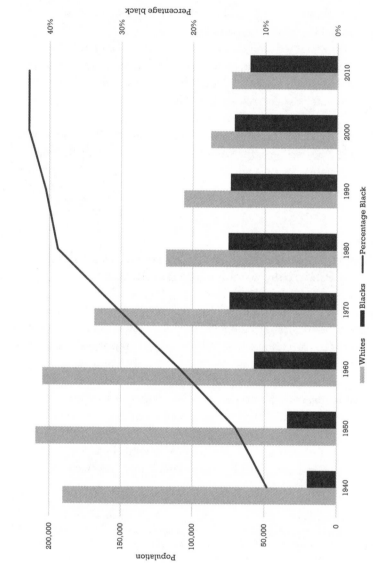

FIGURE 3. Dayton's population by race, 1940–2010. Data notes: 1940 black population refers to nonwhite population, not just black. But only 122 people in 1950 were nonwhite and nonblack in Dayton, and that number was likely trivial in 1940 as well. The approximate 1980 white population = total population – black population (Steven R. Howe et al., "The Shrinking Central City amidst Growing Suburbs: Case Studies of Ohio's Elastic Cities," *Urban Geography* 19, no. 8 [1998]: 714–34).

ing seven-year terms.[13] Lacking a professional planning staff of their own, the board contracted with the Technical Advisory Corporation of New York City in 1924 to create the city's first comprehensive plan. A primary goal of the plan was to create a transportation system that would enable the efficient movement of cars throughout the city.

This plan called for wider streets and a new parkway built over the abandoned portion of the Miami and Erie Canal that ran through the city. The plan was expanded in 1930 and again called for more car-centric road construction that widened streets and eliminated dead ends. Patterson Boulevard was completed over the unused canal in 1939 (with help from some WPA subsidies), and buses began replacing railed streetcars in 1933, though streetcars wouldn't completely leave the city until 1947. As in other cities, the automobile became the focus of Dayton's transportation plans in the 1920s and '30s.

Other areas of the country went through similar changes. Construction of limited-access highways took off in the 1920s in and around New York City. The Bronx River Parkway was dedicated in 1925, and it was followed by the Westchester County parkway system and the Long Island parkways. These parkways had designated entry and exit points and served as a model for the larger interstate highway system that was to come.

The federal Interregional Highway Committee published a report in 1944 that contained what would become the basic layout of the interstate system. That same year, the interstate highway system was officially created with an initial scope of 40,000 miles. Over the next two years, the federal Bureau of Public Roads and the state highway departments laid out routes for the interstates. In 1947 official routes for nearly 38,000 of the 40,000 miles were published. Routes for the remaining miles, largely in and around urban areas, were delayed until more detailed, local information could be gathered.

Despite all this planning, it would be nearly ten years before funding would be obtained and actual construction began. In the early 1950s, a national defense rational was added to the previous pro-highway arguments of alleviating congestion and revitalizing central cities. President Dwight Eisenhower, fresh off his time as supreme commander of the Allied Forces during World War II, had seen firsthand how the German autobahns had enabled the German military to move quickly over land. This experience, coupled with his participation in a 1919 military convoy that crossed the United States by land from Washington, DC, to San Francisco, convinced him that a system of high-speed, connected roads was a necessary compo-

---

13. Dunham, *Dayton, 84.*

nent of military readiness.[14] As a result, he supported federal funding for the highway system, and in 1956 he signed the Federal Aid Highway Act, which secured 90% federal funding for the interstate highway system. The other 10% was to be picked up by the states.

Construction of the highway system was predicted to take approximately 10 years and cost the federal government $27 billion. However, subsequent acts added to the total mileage and this, combined with stricter design standards, environmental considerations, and other issues, resulted in federal payments of approximately $120 billion.[15] It also took nearly 40 years to build. The system as laid out in the 1956 legislation is largely complete, though several urban portions were abandoned or left incomplete due to local opposition, including I-40 in Memphis, I-70 in Baltimore, and I-95 in Washington, DC.

As noted previously, the Interregional Highway Committee's report had a large influence on the highway system, and one of its recommendations that particularly impacted cities like Dayton was that the new highways should pass near cities' central business districts. State and local officials had a similar idea, but on a smaller scale. After World War II, many cities developed urban plans that included extensive highway systems as well as expansions of mass transit such as passenger rail and bus lines.

However, the highways in the city plans were more modest—two lanes each way with 45 to 50 miles-per-hour speed limits—than the highways that bisect America's cities today. But these municipal plans were never fully implemented. Instead, many city officials chose to conserve local revenues and relinquish primary responsibility for large-scale investment to state highway departments, which prioritized faster interstate travel and as a result built the larger system we see today.[16]

As mentioned previously, there was some local opposition in large cities such as Boston, New York, New Orleans, and San Francisco. For highways to pass near central business districts, some homes and businesses had to be torn down. Soon-to-be-displaced property owners understandably objected, and their collective protests led to the Highway Act of 1962, which required that highway construction projects in cities with more than 50,000 people be

14. David A. Pfeiffer, "Ike's Interstates at 50," Prologue Magazine 38, no. 2 (2006), https://www.archives.gov/publications/prologue/2006/summer/interstates.html.

15. "Interstate Frequently Asked Questions," US Department of Transportation, accessed February 1, 2019, https://www.fhwa.dot.gov/interstate/faq.cfm#question6. Both amounts are in nominal dollars.

16. David W. Jones Jr., Urban Transit Policy: An Economic and Political History (Englewood Cliffs, NJ: Prentice Hall, 1985), 69.

constructed in cooperation with local communities. In practice this act didn't have much of an effect on actual highway construction, though as previously mentioned residents in a few cities were able to thwart construction of some portions of city highways.[17]

Dayton, however, was not one of those cities. Interstate 75 runs north-south right through Dayton and follows the Old Dixie Highway—a series of roads completed in 1927 that connected the Midwest to Florida. Interstate 75 runs from Miami, Florida, to Sault Ste. Marie, Michigan, passing through several large cities, including Tampa, Atlanta, Knoxville, Lexington, Cincinnati, and Detroit. The portion of I-75 that runs through Dayton was completed in 1966. Another interstate, I-70, runs east-west and is located approximately 16 miles north of downtown Dayton. It's connected to I-75 on the east side of the city by Interstate 675, which was authorized by the state in 1962 but not completed until 1986.

The construction of I-75 through Dayton's core permanently altered the neighborhoods in its path. Many houses were razed in a residential area on the west side of downtown, from Wilkinson Street to the Miami River, to make room for the highway. A few years later the area was designated an urban renewal area and the rest of the housing was demolished.[18] It eventually became a commercial area, with hotels and office buildings, forcing the displaced residents to find housing elsewhere. Today the area consists of government buildings and Sinclair Community College. Interstate 75 and urban renewal had a similar effect on neighborhoods on the city's west side as well, such as the neighborhood south of 5th Street and north of Washington Street. In the 1940s and '50s it was primarily residential, while today it is primarily commercial and industrial. A comparison of the aerial views of Dayton in photos 4 and 8 (see pages 62 and 66) shows the extent of the residential displacement due to I-75. This direct displacement contributed to Dayton's declining population.

Even though there was some direct displacement, Dayton officials were not concerned at the time about a highway cutting right through the city. In fact, like many other city officials and residents, they believed that the highways would bring suburban residents downtown to shop and work, and that this positive effect would outweigh any negative effects such as migration from the city.[19] But the actual effect turned out to be the opposite of their expectations. Economist Nathaniel Baum-Snow estimates that

---

17. Ellis, "Interstate Highways," 261.

18. Dunham, *Dayton*, 91.

19. Dunham, *Dayton*, 85.

on average the construction of one interstate highway through a central city caused an 18% drop in that city's population between 1950 and 1990.[20] The economic explanation is that the highway decreased the time to commute a given distance, which allowed people to live farther away from the city. Furthermore, the decrease in the price of commuting freed up money that could be used on other things, including more space. And since people really value space—think about how the average home size changes with income—this increased the demand for space and led to more suburbanization and a decline in population density as people consumed more land and built bigger homes.

The highway story of urban decline fits the facts in Dayton. Kettering, Vandalia, Moraine, and Huber Heights all lie along I-75, and each grew rapidly during construction of I-75 in the '50s and early '60s and after its completion in 1966, as shown in table 2. Unlike the other cities, Kettering was already large enough to be incorporated—which occurred in 1955—by the time the interstate highway system was being built. Interstate 75 facilitates access to the most southwestern portion of Kettering and contributed to its growth from the late 1960s until 1970, at which point its population began to decline. Several other suburban communities, such as Centerville, Bellbrook, and Beavercreek, lie along I-675 and they also experienced rapid growth. The large population increases in these suburban communities from 1960 to 1990 support the story that highways contributed to urban decline and suburban growth in the Dayton area.

People weren't the only thing leaving Dayton. Rike's Department Store was one of those iconic, mid-twentieth-century department stores that you can only see in old movies today. It carried everything—clothing, toys, candy, cookware, sporting goods, appliances, bedding, and more. The original dry-goods store opened in Dayton in 1853, and over the next 60 years it moved a few times before settling in at what became its flagship downtown location at the corner of Second Street and Main Street in 1912.[21] It's Christmas window displays appeared in 1945 and were a Dayton favorite that drew in shoppers from all over the region. The displays, originally owned by NCR, appeared in the company's New York City office until Frederik Rike, owner of Rike's, convinced NCR to move them to his store in Dayton.[22]

20. Nathaniel Baum-Snow, "Did Highways Cause Suburbanization?," Quarterly Journal of Economics 122, no. 2 (May 2007): 775–805.

21. "MS-189 Rike's Historical Collection," Wright State University, accessed February 1, 2019, https://www.libraries.wright.edu/special/collectionguides/files/ms189.pdf.

22. Lisa Powell, "Windows into Christmas Past," myDayton Daily News, December 15, 2015, http://www.mydaytondailynews.com/lifestyles/holiday/windows-into-christmas -past/lFt9xWW4NYlogZd9tJuGpK/.

TABLE 2. Population of Dayton's suburbs, 1940–2000

YEAR	FAIRBORN	BEAVERCREEK	KETTERING	VANDALIA	CENTERVILLE	OAKWOOD	BELLBROOK	MORAINE	HUBER HEIGHTS
1940				378	561	7,652	410		
1950	7,847	5,327[a]	38,118[b]	927	827	9,691	425		1,921[c]
1960	19,453	10,315[a]	54,462	6,342	3,490	10,493	941	2,262	12,022[c]
1970	32,267	26,555	69,599	10,796	10,333	10,095	1,268	4,898	18,943
1980	29,747	31,589	61,223	13,161	18,886	9,372	5,174	5,325	34,642
1990	31,300	33,626	60,569	13,882	21,082	8,957	6,511	5,985	38,696
2000	32,052	37,984	57,502	14,603	23,024	9,215	7,009	6,897	38,212

[a] Population data for Beavercreek township prior to the formation of Beavercreek the city.
[b] Kettering's population at its time of incoporation in 1955.
[c] The population of Wayne Township before it incorporated as Huber Heights.

The popularity of the Christmas displays did not blind the owners of Rike's to the changing population patterns, and in 1961 they opened their first branch store in Kettering.[23] The success of that store delayed a planned expansion of the downtown store so that the owners could channel their resources to additional suburban stores. They opened two additional stores: one in 1963 on a site that would become the Salem Mall a few years later and another in 1969 at the brand-new Dayton Mall, which despite its name is actually located in Miami Township, outside of Dayton's city limits.

Despite its expansion and early success in the suburbs, Rike's remained committed to its downtown store. However, sales kept declining and the downtown location closed in 1991, though at the time of its closure it was under a new name, Lazarus, having merged with the Columbus-based chain in 1986. The building was razed eight years later to make room for the Benjamin and Marian Schuster Performing Arts Center, which today displays the old Rike's Christmas displays in its lobby windows during the holidays.

Other stores followed Rike's to the suburbs. Donenfeld's, a men's and women's clothing store, opened a store in the Salem Mall in 1966 and in the Dayton Mall in 1970. From 1967 to 1982, downtown's share of the metropolitan area's retail sales fell from 12.3% to only 3.7%, and the merchants' hopes that the highways would bring people downtown declined along with their sales.[24]

In addition to the highways, government housing polices also helped suburban areas grow at the expense of cities. The Federal Housing Administration (FHA), created in 1934 as part of FDR's New Deal, used federal dollars to insure mortgage loans, which made mortgages relatively safe and profitable investments. Due to its large financial stake in the housing market, the FHA came to drive community planning standards.[25] The FHA underwriting guidelines favored loans in less built-up, often suburban locations, noting, "Interior locations have a tendency to exhibit a gradual decline in quality."[26]

The FHA, in combination with the 1944 Veterans Affairs (VA) home-loan program, also helped decrease the down payment required to purchase a home and helped increase the length of a mortgage. In the early twenti-

---

23. Dunham, *Dayton*, 86.

24. Dunham, *Dayton*, 88.

25. Tom Hanchett, "The Other 'Subsidized Housing': Federal Aid to Suburbanization, 1940s—1960s," in *From Tenements to Taylor Homes: In Search of Urban Housing Policy in Twentieth Century America, ed.* Roger Biles and Kristin Szylvian (*University Park:* Pennsylvania State University Press, 2000), 163–79.

26. Hanchett, "Subsidized Housing," 2

eth century, buyers typically had to put down 50% of a home's purchase price and then either pay off the balance after five (sometimes ten) years or find a lender willing to refinance the outstanding balance for another five to ten years once the initial mortgage period ended.[27] But due to the FHA-VA mortgage guarantees that decreased banks' risk of losing money, banks began accepting much lower down payments, anywhere from 0% to 10%, and stretched the mortgage out to 30 years.[28] These program criteria quickly became the industry standard and helped increase the percentage of housing units in America that were owner-occupied from around 45% prior to World War II to 62% by 1960.[29]

The FHA-VA programs also incentivized building on a large scale, which pushed capital away from smaller, craft builders to large builders such as William Levitt, the developer of the eponymous Levittown communities in the Mid-Atlantic. The FHA believed large developments promoted construction efficiency and liked that large builders assumed responsibility for planning the communities, developing the land, and selling the finished units.[30]

The planning characteristics preferred by those at the FHA included single-use zoning, curving avenues, and cul-de-sacs, all designed to promote the ideal of private residential life.[31] And as we discussed earlier, until 1950 the FHA also discouraged the mixing of races and different income classes in an effort to maintain neighborhood home values. The FHA's preference for large communities, secluded residential neighborhoods, and racially homogeneous communities pushed development farther away from city centers, including Dayton's, and out to the suburbs where few blacks lived and land was readily available.

The migration of people from cities to the suburbs also impacted the location of businesses. The urban economics version of the chicken-or-the-egg question is whether people moved to the suburbs first and business followed or vice versa. While there are individual cases that support both sequences, the bulk of the evidence suggests that many firms, especially retail and commercial firms, tended to follow people to the suburbs.[32] Many

27. Richard K. Green and Susan M. Wachter, "The American Mortgage in historical and International Context," *Journal of Economic Perspectives* 19, no. 4 (Fall 2005): 93–114.

28. Hanchett, "Subsidized Housing," 2.

29. "Historic Census of Housing Tables," US Census Bureau, revised October 31, 2011, https://www.census.gov/hhes/www/housing/census/historic/owner.html.

30. Hanchett, "Subsidized Housing," 3.

31. Hanchett, "Subsidized Housing," 3.

32. Edward L. Glaeser and Matthew E. Kahn, "Decentralized Employment and the Transformation of the American City," *Brookings-Wharton Papers on Urban Affairs* 2001, no. 1 (2001): 1–63; Jason Barr and Troy Tassier, "The Dynamics of Subcenter Formation:

people left the city to buy bigger houses, to evade mandatory busing, and to avoid the social problems and subsequent tax increases associated with poorer southern migrants. The firms that relied on these people as both employees and customers, such as Rike's, followed.

The dispersion of residents and firms from city centers to their surrounding suburbs in the latter half of the twentieth century, a process referred to as decentralization, was especially large in manufacturing cities such as Dayton. According to one study, by the mid-1990s the Dayton-Springfield metro area was the most decentralized metro area in the Midwest.[33]

Economists have traditionally modeled cities as being monocentric. That is, a city has a center—the central business district—that contains most of the jobs and people live around the center. The density of buildings and their price decline as one gets farther from the center to compensate for the longer commuting time and higher commuting costs.

The monocentric layout of cities arose due to the importance of water as a means of transporting goods and people. Before trains and later automobiles became important modes of transportation, people relied on rivers, lakes, and oceans to traverse long distances. Horse and buggy were used for personal transportation and last-mile shipping, but ships were used to move people and goods from city to city due to their speed and lower cost. The importance of water transportation can be seen by the locations of many of the largest midwestern cities: Chicago, Detroit, Cleveland, Buffalo, Pittsburgh, Cincinnati, St. Louis, Milwaukee, and Dayton are all located along the Great Lakes or navigable rivers.

The lower cost of water transportation was more important to firms shipping heavy agricultural commodities and manufactured goods than to individual people, so firms outbid people for land along water, and downtowns filled up with factories, warehouses, and shops instead of houses and apartment buildings. People lived on the outskirts of the central business district, and initially most of them lived within walking distance. With the advent of streetcars and trolleys, people moved farther from city centers to avoid the din and dirt of the factories and warehouses.

Trains reduced the importance of water transportation, but within cities they tended to follow established routes along rivers and canals and thus they didn't have much of an effect on the monocentric layout of the city. It

Midtown Manhattan, 1861–1906," *Journal of Regional Science* 56, no. 5 (2016): 754–91. For an alternative explanation, especially in regard to manufacturing, see Robert Bruegmann, *Sprawl: A Compact History* (Chicago: University of Chicago Press, 2005).

33. Glaeser and Kahn, "Decentralized Employment," 12.

wasn't until cars and trucks came into widespread use that businesses and people began to significantly fan out from the center. The creation of the interstate highway system further lowered the cost of commuting to the urban center and accelerated the decentralization process in Dayton and other midwestern cities.

As the United States lost its dominance over manufacturing during the last half of the twentieth century, the factories and warehouses that had sprung up many decades earlier in the central business districts of cities like Dayton closed and the surrounding neighborhoods began to decay. We will discuss this more in the next section.

The Importance of Human Capital and the Decline of Manufacturing

Perhaps the most consistent factor associated with population growth in cities is human capital. Human capital is the stock of skills that people possess. Since skills such as intelligence, creativity, and work ethic are hard to measure, economists often use educational attainment as a proxy for human capital. Economists have found that cities with a high proportion of educated residents—that is, cities with a lot of human capital—regularly grow faster than similar cities with fewer educated residents.[34] This relationship can be seen in figure 4, which shows the share of the city's population age 25 or older with a bachelor's degree or more in 1967 and the population growth of that city from 1970 to 2017 for 30 large US cities.[35] Cold-weather cities—those with average January temperature below 40 degrees—are identified with black squares.

As shown in figure 4, there is a positive relationship between education and population growth for the 30 cities as a group and for the cold cities on their own. It's also a relatively strong relationship: The share of the adult population with a bachelor's degree or more explains 29% of the variation in population growth in this sample. Only a few of the cold-weather cities

34. Edward L. Glaeser and Albert Saiz, "*The Rise of the Skilled City*" (Working Paper No. 10191, National Bureau of Economic Research, 2003); Edward L. Glaeser, "Cities, Information, and Economic Growth," *Cityscape* 1, no. 1 (1994): 9–47.

35. US Census Bureau, https://www.census.gov/content/census/en/data/tables/1967/demo/educational-attainment/p20-209.html. I used the central city share of residents with a bachelor's degree or more as my x-variable and the city—not metro area—population growth as my y-variable.

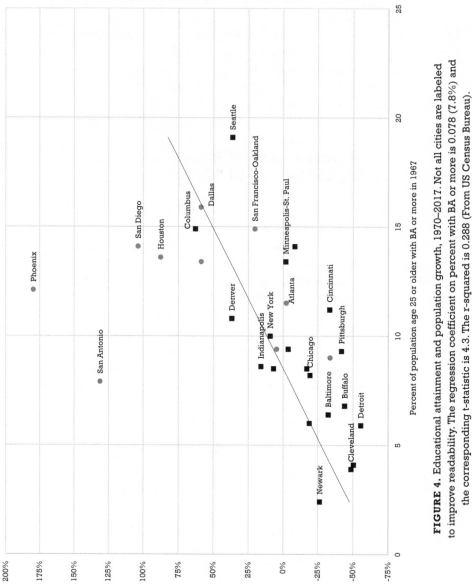

FIGURE 4. Educational attainment and population growth, 1970–2017. Not all cities are labeled to improve readability. The regression coefficient on percent with BA or more is 0.078 (7.8%) and the corresponding t-statistic is 4.3. The r-squared is 0.288 (From US Census Bureau).

gained population while the rest of them shrank by various amounts, but regardless of the amount of growth, this is evidence that a high percentage of educated residents can at least dampen subsequent population decline.

There is a large literature that shows that a highly educated population contributes to economic and population growth in cities when controlling for other factors.[36] In one study, economists Duncan Black and Vernon Henderson develop a growth model supported by evidence from US metropolitan area data that shows that human capital accumulation positively impacts metro area population growth.[37] Economist Curtis Simon also finds a robust, positive relationship between levels of human capital within a metro area and employment growth.[38] More importantly, Simon provides evidence that the economic benefits of human capital on growth are at least partly localized within a city's boundaries. This means that politicians who are interested in stemming population decline in cities like Dayton may be able to do so by attracting high human capital individuals to their city from the surrounding metro area.

There are several theoretical explanations for why a large proportion of high-skill workers leads to more population and economic growth: High-skill workers increase the growth rate of entrepreneurs; they increase the demand for non-tradeable goods (e.g., restaurant meals and personal services) due to their higher incomes and this creates business opportunities for people who provide such goods; and populations with a lot of human capital are better able to overcome adverse economic shocks.[39]

Earlier we saw that only 8% of Dayton's residents had a college degree in 1958. This number was likely lower by 1967 as poorer, less-educated southern migrants continued to move into Dayton and educated Dayton natives moved to suburban communities such as Beavercreek and Center-

36. Edward L. Glaeser, Giacomo A. M. Ponzetto, and Kristina Tobio, "Cities, Skills and Regional Change," *Regional Studies* 48, no. 1 (2014): 7–43; C. Nardinelli and C. J. Simon, "The Talk of the Town: Human Capital, Information, and the Growth of English Cities, 1861 to 1961," Explorations in Economic History 33, no. 3 (1996) 384–413; C. Nardinelli and C. J. Simon, "Human Capital and the Rise of American Cities, 1900–1990," Regional Science and Urban Economics 32 (2002): 59–96.

37. Duncan Black and Vernon Henderson, "A Theory of Urban Growth," *Journal of Political Economy* 107, no. 2 (1999): 252–84.

38. Curtis Simon, "Human Capital and Metropolitan Employment Growth," Journal of Urban Economics 43, no. 2 (March 1998): 223–43.

39. Glaeser, Ponzetto, and Tobio, "Regional change"; Enrico Moretti, "Local Multipliers," American Economic Review 100, no. 2 (2010): 373–77; Glaeser and Saiz, "Rise of the Skilled City," 47–105. For an example, see Edward L. Glaeser, "Reinventing Boston: 1630–2003," *Journal of Economic Geography* 5, no. 2 (2005): 119–53.

ville.[40] Even under the assumption that the share of residents with a bachelor's degree or more held steady at 8%, Dayton would have been in the southwest quadrant of figure 4. Only two cold-weather cities, Boston and Indianapolis, grew from 1970 to 2017 with such a low percentage of college educated residents in 1967.

Many of the migrants to Montgomery County during World War II and the early 1950s came to take factory jobs that required little formal education. In 1959, of the residents who had lived in Montgomery County for five to 19 years—those who migrated between 1940 and 1954—47% had less than a high school education versus 17% who had at least one year of college.[41] The newer migrants of the late 1950s had more education than earlier migrants on average: In 1959, only 38% of adult residents who had lived in Montgomery County for fewer than five years had less than a high school education, compared to 31% who had at least one year of college. Unfortunately for Dayton, the more educated people arriving in Montgomery County in the late 1950s were also more likely to settle outside of Dayton than those arriving in the 1940s. As shown earlier, the populations of Kettering, Vandalia, and Huber Heights all grew rapidly during this period and the percentage of Montgomery County residents who lived in Dayton declined.

The Great Migration from the rural South to the industrial North also had an unfavorable effect on the composition of Dayton's labor force due to the lack of educational opportunities in the South for blacks. In a 1973 study, economist Finis Welch found that in the 1920s and '30s southern schools spent about three times more on white students than on black students.[42] Southern black schools were also in session significantly fewer days on average than all southern schools—119 days versus 162 in the 1919–20 school year—and the average days attended per enrolled student was significantly lower in southern black schools than all southern schools—80 days versus 121.[43] The black migrants to Ohio from 1920 to 1930 largely came from Kentucky, Georgia, Tennessee, and Alabama;[44] the latter three are former Confederate states where school segregation was institutionalized and thus the

40. In 1970, 11.2% of Montgomery County residents 25 and older had a bachelor's degree or more, very close to the 10% in 1958 as reported in table 1. If the college-educated ratio of Dayton to Montgomery County was steady over this time period, we would expect approximately 9% of Dayton's residents to have had a bachelor's degree or more in 1970.

41. *Metropolitan Challenge.*

42. Finis Welch, "Black-White Differences in Returns to Schooling," *American Economic Review* 63, no. 5 (December 1973): 893–907.

43. Welch, "Black-White Differences," 900.

44. See table 1 in Carrington, Detragiache, and Vishwanath, "Moving Costs."

characteristics of black schools in these states were likely to align with the low averages presented in Welch's study.

Other researchers have also noted that southern blacks typically attended low-quality schools, and as a result they tended to be less productive workers. Even after migrating to the North, black workers were better substitutes for contemporaneous European immigrants than American-born, northern-educated whites due to the European group's similar subpar education in lower-quality southern and eastern European schools.[45]

These numbers imply that the human capital of Dayton's labor force was actually lower in the mid-twentieth century than what is implied by table 2. The educational attainment of Dayton's population is reported in that table, but the data says nothing about the quality of the education. Given the study by Welch, it's likely that people with an eighth grade education or less and those with some high school but no degree in Dayton in 1958 had even less human capital than what those relatively low levels of education suggest. The same is probably true for high school graduates as well.

As stated earlier, by 1960 nearly 20% of Dayton's population was black, and many of them were black migrants from southern states in the Deep South that had low-quality black schools. Southern black schools improved relative to white schools after 1920, but even as late as 1949–50 they significantly lagged white schools in number of days in session, average days attended, and per student spending.[46] All of this suggests that many of the southern black migrants who arrived in Dayton from 1940 to 1970 had less human capital than the official education statistics indicate.[47]

The low amounts of human capital possessed by the black migrants combined with the out-migration of highly educated white northerners caused the total amount of human capital within the city of Dayton to decline. In this way, the legal racial discrimination that existed in the South and impeded the human capital accumulation of blacks ultimately impacted northern cities such as Dayton. The influx of low-skill workers combined with the outflow of high-skill workers meant a dearth of human capital that negatively affected Dayton's ability to innovate and adapt, contributing to the city's decline during the latter half of the twentieth century.

---

45. Boustan, *Competition*, 4.

46. See table 3 in Welch, "Black-White Differences."

47. Gyourko makes a similar point in his discussion of Philadelphia in the early twentieth century. See Joseph Gyourko, Robert A. Margo, and Andrew F. Haughwout. "Looking Back to Look Forward: Learning from Philadelphia's 350 Years of Urban Development [with Comments]." *Brookings-Wharton Papers on Urban Affairs* (2005): 1–58.

In addition to the demand-side reasons for the lack of residents with a college degree, there is also a supply-side reason—the lack of colleges in the area in the early twentieth century. Firms often rely on nearby universities to create a pool of talented workers from which to hire. Today there are three traditional brick-and-mortar schools of higher learning in the Dayton area: the University of Dayton (UD), Wright State University, and Sinclair Community College. But prior to 1960, only the private University of Dayton existed. As for the public universities, Wright State was established in 1967 and Sinclair opened for classes in 1972.[48] Thus, in the years immediately following World War II when a large number of former GIs were attending college and enrollments in general were increasing, Dayton had only one small private university to offer potential students.

In 1946 there were only 2,800 students on UD's campus, though enrollment increased to 8,700 by 1964–65.[49] Yet despite this growth, the number of students enrolled in college in the Dayton area was small compared to other nearby Ohio cities. The Ohio State University in Columbus had an enrollment of nearly 26,000 in 1950 and the University of Cincinnati's enrollment was nearly 14,000 that same year.[50] This supply-side factor also harmed Dayton's ability to innovate since the city was not producing many residents with high human capital.

In the latter half of the twentieth century, the Dayton area failed to remain the innovative area it had once been. A study that examined the geographic location of research and development (R & D) labs and employment in 1975 shows that Dayton was outside of the top 20 metro areas in terms of total number of R & D labs and employment.[51] The Dayton metro area placed in the top 20 in only one area, the location of federally employed scientists and engineers, due to Wright-Patterson Air Force Base. A report by the US Patent and Trademark Office, which used 1998 data, showed that the

48. Sinclair's origin goes back to a YMCA college established in the late nineteenth century that later became a private two-year college. This small college was vastly different in both form and purpose compared to today's Sinclair Community College in downtown Dayton and as such had a negligible effect on educating Dayton's population.

49. Kay Timmons, "University of Dayton: Potential Unlimited," Dayton History Books, originally printed in *Dayton USA*, September 1965, http://www.daytonhistory-books.com/page/page/4706308.htm.

50. "The Ohio State University," Ohio History Central, accessed February 4, 2019, http://www.ohiohistorycentral.org/w/The_Ohio_State_University; "Overview of the History of the University of Cincinnati," University of Cincinnati, accessed February 4, 2019, https://www.uc.edu/content/dam/uc/af/pdc/campus_heritage_plan/new_heritage_files/Chapter%202%20(4.4mb).pdf.

51. Edward J. Malecki, "Dimensions of R & D Location in the United States," *Research Policy* 9, no. 1 (1980): 2–22.

Dayton-Springfield metro area generated 20.4 patents per 100,000 people, a rate that left it well out of the top 30 and below the national rate of 60 patents per 100,000 people.[52] This is a sharp contrast to Dayton's aforementioned patent output in the early 1900s, when the city of Dayton was generating roughly 120 patents per 100,000 people.

Theoretical work on economic growth in the 1990s formalized the mechanism by which research and development impacts a region's economic growth.[53] In these models, ideas beget ideas and economic output expands as entrepreneurs bring these ideas to the market. As we discussed earlier, economist Joseph Schumpeter introduced the idea of "creative destruction," a process that involves the endless introduction of new and better products that then destroy the profit margins of older goods and services. Research and development is a critical component of this process, and firms that fail to innovate will be overtaken by their competitors.

In addition to businesses, large research universities are an important source of R & D. The knowledge generated at research-intensive universities often spills over into the surrounding economy and this leads to higher wages for local workers in other noneducation industries.[54] Workers employed in industries that hire a lot of local graduates and that have commercial uses for the knowledge created by local universities typically benefit the most.

A healthy relationship between firms and universities is important for a city's success. Not only do universities provide a pool of educated workers but their research activity often directly impacts firms' bottom lines. Former GM president Alfred Sloan recognized the importance of university research and believed that "since the outcome of basic research is the foundation of the knowledge used in industry, it is appropriate and an expression of enlightened self-interest for industry to make outside grants to universities for basic research."[55] In return, universities who commercialize faculty research in partnership with private firms can earn a significant sum of

52. "United States Patent Grants: Number of Grants per 100,000 Population, by Metropolitan Area, 1998," US Patent and Trademark Office, http://www.uspto.gov/web/offices/ac/ido/oeip/taf/pc98_all.pdf.

53. Paul M. Romer, "Endogenous Technological Change," *Journal of Political Economy* (1990): S71–S102; Charles I. Jones, "R & D-based Models of Economic Growth," *Journal of Political Economy* 103, no. 4 (August 1995): 759–84.

54. Shawn Kantor and Alexander Whalley, "Knowledge Spillovers from Research Universities: Evidence from Endowment Value Shocks," *Review of Economics and Statistics* 96, no. 1 (2014): 171–88.

55. Sloan, *My Years*, 251.

money that can be used to hire additional faculty, create student scholar-
ships, or maintain or build facilities, among other things.

However, not all universities are able to make such a relationship work
since not all universities focus on research. The Carnegie Classification of
Institutions of Higher Education separates universities into several different categories based on their research activity, types of degrees conferred,
and course offerings. For example, research universities are separated into
three categories. Universities with the highest level of research activity are
classified as R1, and there are 115 of them in the United States.[56] In addition to R1 universities, there are 107 US universities classified as R2, where
higher research activity takes place, and 112 classified as R3, which engages
in moderate research activity. The 222 R1 and R2 universities are a small
percentage of the roughly 2,800 four-year US colleges and universities, but
they are the schools primarily responsible for the knowledge spillovers that
generate higher wages. The R1 universities in Ohio include Ohio State, Case
Western, and the University of Cincinnati. As for the universities in the Dayton area, the University of Dayton is an R2 university and Wright State is
an R3.

The relatively low research output of the Dayton area universities can be
seen in the patent data. During the latter half of the twentieth century, the
major universities in the Dayton area produced fewer patents than several
other Ohio universities. From 1969 to 2000, the University of Dayton and
Wright State produced 77 and 46 utility patents respectively, which ranked
sixth and seventh among Ohio universities.[57] Unsurprisingly, The Ohio State
University—the largest in the state—had the most utility patents over this
period, followed by the University of Akron, Case Western Reserve University, the University of Cincinnati, and the University of Toledo. Even
the combined patent output of the University of Dayton and Wright State
only placed fourth, just in front of the University of Cincinnati but behind
Case Western and the University of Akron. The lack of a large, productive
research university in Dayton hindered the city's ability to innovate during
the latter half of the twentieth century compared to other cities.

The importance of universities becomes even more relevant once we
consider how knowledge spreads. Most knowledge is easily transmitted
across large distances via academic journals, newspapers, books, radio, TV,

56. "News and Announcements," Carnegie Classification of Institutions of Higher
Education, accessed September 2017, http://carnegieclassifications.iu.edu/index.php.

57. "US Colleges and Universities: Utility Patent Grants, 1969–2012," US Patent and
Trademark Office, https://www.uspto.gov/web/offices/ac/ido/oeip/taf/univ/org_
grx/t250_univ_agx.htm.

and, more recently, the internet. The spread of new, cutting-edge knowledge, however, often relies on face-to-face contact. Before new knowledge is published in an academic journal or reported in a newspaper, it is a paper on a researcher's desk or a file stored on a computer. Having access to such knowledge before it's made public can give a firm an advantage in the marketplace, which is why local, interpersonal connections between firms and universities are so important. As economist Shahid Yusuf puts it, "Knowledge circulation is a 'full-contact sport' and people need to be able to meet face-to-face for a network to function and for any meaningful exchange of uncodified knowledge to occur."[58] Industry-university networks can also facilitate hiring and improve the quality of employee-employer matches. For example, it was one of Edward Deeds's former professors who recommended Charles Kettering for Deeds's open position in the inventions department at NCR.[59]

The importance of R & D doesn't mean that Dayton would have thrived throughout the twentieth century if only it had a large research university like Ohio State. In his case study of Boston, economist Edward Glaeser discusses Boston's transformation from a city built on the shipping and fishing industries to one specializing in the information and technology industries, which form the backbone of the modern knowledge economy. He attributes part of Boston's ability to reinvent itself to its nearby universities such as the Massachusetts Institute of Technology, Harvard, Boston College, and several others. Yet despite these and other universities, Boston still experienced periods of decline, most notably from 1920 to 1980 when its population fell from over 750,000 to 563,000. Universities play an important role in a city's long-term success by facilitating innovation, but their presence alone doesn't mean a city will avoid tough times.

The Decline of Manufacturing

The lack of innovative firms and universities in the Dayton area in the latter half of the twentieth century contributed to Dayton's waning economy. Throughout the twentieth century Dayton relied on the inventions and achievements of its past: NCR, Frigidaire, Delco, Mead Corporation, McCall's, Huffy Corporation, and L. M. Berry were all well-known national companies and significant employers in the Dayton region through the latter

---

58. Shahid Yusuf, "Intermediating Knowledge Exchange between Universities and Businesses," *Research Policy* 37, no. 8 (September 2008): 1173.

59. Marcosson, *Colonel Deeds*, 87.

half of the century, and each was started prior to 1940. After the entrepreneurs and innovators of the early 1900s passed away—Charles Kettering, John Patterson, and others—new innovators failed to take their place. As a result, Dayton became dependent on a handful of historically large employers to provide an economic base for the city.

One of these companies was General Motors, whose relationship with Dayton began in the early twentieth century. General Motors was started by William C. Durant, who was working for the Buick Motor Company at the time.[60] Prior to his time at Buick, Durant was a leading carriage and wagon producer. But like Henry Ford, Durant believed that the automobile would replace the horse-drawn wagon and every household would own one.

The rise of the automobile, however, was not obvious at the time. In the early 1900s cars were unreliable, uncomfortable, and noisy, and there were few decent roads on which to drive them. But this didn't deter Durant. In 1908 he incorporated the General Motors Company and quickly turned it into an automobile conglomerate by purchasing car manufacturers Buick and Olds (later Oldsmobile) in 1908 and Cadillac and Oakland (later Pontiac) in 1909. These companies were subsidiaries under the parent General Motors Company and retained most of their independence.

Durant was a better visionary and creator than manager, and he was forced out of active management of General Motors in 1910. But this wasn't the end of his career in the automobile industry. He then cofounded the Chevrolet Motor Company with Louis Chevrolet and used this company to regain control of GM in 1916. Shortly after, Durant turned the General Motors Company, which was a holding company, into the General Motors Corporation. The former independent subsidiaries—Buick, Cadillac, for example—became operating divisions within the General Motors Corporation. Chevrolet was added in 1918.

It was during the period 1918 to 1920 that GM began its relationship with Dayton. In 1918 Durant bought the Guardian Frigerator Company of Detroit. This company, which was eventually headquartered in the Dayton area, was the basis for the Frigidaire division of GM, which made home appliances such as refrigerators, washing machines, and ranges. Also in 1918 GM acquired Delco when it bought the United Motors Company, which had purchased Delco in 1916. Then in 1919 GM purchased three other Dayton area companies: Domestic Engineering Company, Dayton Metal Products Company, and Dayton Wright Airplane Company. Except for the Guardian

60. Sloan, *My Years*, 3.

Frigerator Company, each of these companies was cofounded by Charles Kettering and Edward Deeds.

The acquisitions of Kettering's and Deeds' companies gave GM a large presence in Dayton's labor market and gave the city a reputation as a "GM town." In fact, Dayton was such a GM town that Ford used it to gauge the demand for the Ford Mustang. The Mustang was released in 1964 and early sales far outpaced planned production. In his autobiography, Lee Iaccoca, former president of the Ford Motor Company, reports that then Ford marketing manager Frank Zimmerman devised an experiment to see just how popular the Mustang really was.[61] Zimmerman believed that if the Mustang could sell in Dayton, then it really must be in demand. As stated by Iacocca:

> He [Zimmerman] met with the Ford dealers in Dayton and told them: "Look, you guys are in a tough, competitive market here, and the Mustang's a hot car. We want to see how hot it really is, so we're going to give each of you ten cars to put in stock and we'll honor your retail orders as quickly as you get them." The results were amazing. We got something like ten percent of the entire car market in Dayton.

While the success of the Mustang might have cut into GM's sales in the Dayton area, it didn't do much to diminish GM's role as an employer. As late as 1980, employment in the Dayton metro area was still largely tied to GM and the automotive industry as a result of GM's earlier purchases of Kettering's and Deeds' businesses. One study reports that the Dayton metro area contained 11 automotive-related plants that employed 41,800 workers in 1980, which was over 43% of the metro area's manufacturing employment and just over 10% of all nonfarm employment.[62]

Cities where employment is heavily concentrated in one firm or industry tend to be less dynamic and innovative and this hurts long-term economic growth. As we discussed previously, high-human capital workers are important for economic growth because of their ability to generate new ideas and adapt to changing economic circumstances. New ideas are often generated by workers talking and sharing knowledge with one another, and such knowledge sharing can take place two different ways: workers can share knowledge with other workers within their same industry or workers can share knowledge with workers outside of their industry.

---

61. Lee Iacocca, *Iacocca: An Autobiography* (New York: Bantam Books, 1984), 79.

62. Carol MacLennan and J. O'Donnell, "The Effects of the Automotive Transition on Employment: A Plant and Community Study" (Third Automotive Fuel Economy Research Contractor's Coordination Meeting, US DOT, NHTSA, December 1–2, 1980).

Within-industry knowledge sharing occurs when a high concentration of firms in the same industry facilitates knowledge sharing as workers move from one firm to another and imitate one another's successes. The industry grows due to the innovation and increased specialization that this knowledge sharing generates, and the city grows along with it. A relatively modern example of this phenomenon is computer chips in Silicon Valley. An older example that impacted Dayton was the automobile industry in Detroit in the early 1900s. Entrepreneurs such as Chevrolet, Ford, the Dodge brothers, and Buick were clustered in Detroit, and workers moved freely among the companies, spreading knowledge along the way. The companies mimicked one another's best ideas and in the process helped Detroit become the fifth-largest city in America by 1950.

The second method, across-industry knowledge sharing, involves workers from firms in different industries sharing knowledge with one another. This type of knowledge sharing relies on the proximity of firms in a variety of industries and it generates growth as these across-industry interactions lead to new ideas. The important role that across-industry knowledge sharing can play in urban growth was popularized by urbanist Jane Jacobs.

While both within- and across-industry knowledge sharing can lead to economic growth in theory, the evidence from the latter half of the twentieth century suggests that across-industry knowledge sharing was more important in terms of growth. Cities with more industrial diversity tended to grow faster than cities with more industrial concentration.[63] Dayton's heavy reliance on manufacturing, and GM in particular, limited the opportunities for across-industry knowledge sharing. This stifled innovation in the city and contributed to its decline.

The lack of innovation that contributed to Dayton's employment and population decline that began after 1960 was not an isolated occurrence in the Rust Belt.[64] The region experienced a large decline in employment relative to the rest of the country in the decades following World War II. From 1950 to 2000, the share of total US employment in the Rust Belt declined from 43% to 27%. Over the same period, the region's share of all US manufacturing employment declined from 51% to 33%.[65] Any complex economic event is bound to have several, often overlapping causes. In addition to the

63. Edward L. Glaeser, Hedi D. Kallal, José A. Scheinkman, and Andrei Shleifer, "Growth in Cities," *Journal of Political Economy* 100, no. 6 (1992): 1126–52.

64. Here the Rust Belt includes the states of Wisconsin, Illinois, Indiana, Michigan, Ohio, West Virginia, Pennsylvania, and New York.

65. Simeon Alder, David Lagakos, and Lee Ohanian, "Labor Market Conflict and the Decline of the Rust Belt" (manuscript, University of California, San Diego, 2017).

lack of industrial diversity, conflict between labor unions and management also contributed to the lack of innovation by firms in Dayton and the Rust Belt more broadly.

Two of the largest and most powerful unions in the country are based in the Midwest: the United Steelworkers and the United Auto Workers (UAW). By the 1940s all the big auto companies, including GM, were unionized. One of the primary goals of unions is to increase member's wages and on this front the Rust Belt unions were successful. Manufacturing workers in the Rust Belt made about 13% more than similar workers in other regions from 1950 to 1980.

During this period, unions used the threat of strikes—and actual strikes when necessary—to strengthen their bargaining position and increase members' wages relative to similar, nonunionized workers in other parts of the country. Between 1950 and the late 1970s, there were hundreds of strikes per year involving at least 1,000 workers.[66] While strikes occurred throughout the country, there is evidence that labor-management conflict was more prevalent in midwestern industries, such as automobiles, steel, and rubber, than in other US industries.[67]

Companies such as GM attempted to deal with the perpetual threat of strikes by agreeing to longer-term contracts. GM entered into the first five-year contract with the UAW in 1950 in an effort to alleviate the animosity generated by annual negotiation between labor and management.[68] Other auto companies soon followed suit.

The five-year contract was not the panacea some had hoped for, and the threat of strike remained a constant concern. The auto companies tried other solutions, such as substituting capital for labor—that is, more automation—and moving operations to the South where right-to-work laws precluded compulsory union membership, which the auto companies hoped would help decrease their labor costs. However, in many cases the UAW was able to counter by specifying work rules and job classifications within collective bargaining agreements that protected jobs or by successfully unionizing southern production facilities.[69]

---

66. Alder, Lagakos, and Ohanian, "Labor Market"; see pp. 13–19 for an overview of strike activity from 1950 to 2000.

67. Alder, Lagakos, and Ohanian, "Labor Market." See references therein.

68. Alder, Lagakos, and Ohanian, "Labor Market."

69. Douglas Nelson, "The Political Economy of US Automobile Protection," in *The Political Economy of American Trade Policy*, ed. Anne O. Krueger (University of Chicago Press, 1996), 133–96.

While the union-protected wage premium was beneficial to Rust Belt union members at the time, there is evidence that it imposed long-term costs on the region. In addition to increasing the costs of GM and other area firms relative to their less unionized competitors in other countries and states, union power also had a pernicious effect on innovation and productivity through what economists call a "hold-up" problem.

The hold-up problem arose in the Rust Belt during the postwar period because while firms bore the full cost of innovation, they knew that any increase in profits due to productivity improvements would have to be bargained over with the unions. This made them reluctant to invest, since they knew unions would try to capture as large a share of the new profits as possible and could employ disruptive strikes if necessary. As a result, innovation and worker productivity growth lagged in industries such as automobiles and rubber.

Dayton Press is a good example of this problem. Previously the McCall's Corporation, Dayton Press published and printed magazines. By the mid-1960s, the company employed over 6,000 people at its west side plant in Dayton.[70] However, a six-day strike in 1978 caused the company to miss deadlines, harming its reputation. In 1979 the company asked the unions representing its workers for wage concessions in order to invest in new equipment, but some unions objected and no deal was reached. The company closed in 1981 and laid off its remaining 2,500 workers.

Several other Dayton companies closed in the late 1970s and early 1980s because of a failure to innovate or because production shifted to lower cost areas of the country. Frigidaire, GM's home appliance company, had operated in Dayton since 1920. In the mid-1950s it employed almost 20,000 people, but by 1979 all its Dayton operations were closed.[71] Howard Houser, a former employee of Frigidaire, wrote that the company's decline was in part due to its failure to adapt. Competitors General Electric and Whirlpool had built modern plants and updated their marketing strategies, while GM invested little in plants and equipment and continued to market appliances like cars. In 1979, unable to sell the factories, GM closed them and sold the Frigidaire name and goodwill to Cleveland-based White Consolidated Industries.

In 1980 the Dayton Tire and Rubber Company closed its west-side Riverside Avenue plant, where it had operated since 1917.[72] The Dayton Tire company was bought by Firestone in 1961, and eventually Firestone shifted

---

70. Dunham, *Dayton*, 127.
71. Dunham, *Dayton*, 126.
72. Dunham, *Dayton*, 126.

production to its newer plant in Oklahoma, which manufactured steel-belted radial tires that had less rolling resistance and provided better control at higher speeds than the outdated bias ply tires made in Dayton.

GM didn't go out of business, but like these other companies its economic fortunes declined during the late 1970s through the 1980s. Conflict with unions and increased competition from Asian manufacturers contributed to GM's financial struggles. In 1954 GM was the largest car manufacturer and controlled more than 50% of the US automobile market.[73] During that decade, imports, primarily Volkswagens and European sports cars, made some inroads in America, but GM and other domestic manufacturers were able to regain most of their market share by the early 1960s by producing smaller models that were more competitive with European imports.

However, by the late 1960s Asian companies like Toyota, Honda, and Nissan were rapidly gaining market share. The sales of imported vehicles as a percentage of total sales rose from 9% in 1967 to 27% in 1980.[74] Japanese cars were cheaper to produce, primarily due to lower labor costs, and thus sold for less than their US or European counterparts. They were also widely considered to be more reliable and energy efficient than domestic models, which became especially relevant when oil prices spiked during the latter half of the 1970s.

Yet despite the competition from Asia, GM still grew and invested in new plants. GM built four new assembly plants in the late 1970s and early '80s, though it also closed four other outdated plants. Other domestic auto manufacturers also invested in new plants, as did foreign manufacturers. Many of the new plants were in the Midwest, but the characteristics of the sites changed, and these changes are consistent with the incentives firms faced due to strikes and the hold-up problem.

Instead of locating the new plants in urbanized areas, plants were located in more rural areas. Of the fifteen new plant sites chosen from 1965 to 1986 by all auto manufacturers, only three were in a county that contained a central city of a metropolitan area. In the two decades prior, 12 plants had been built in counties that contained central cities. This shift from urban to rural areas was not in Dayton's favor.

Consistent with the hold-up problem, one reason put forth for this urban-to-rural shift was that auto companies, both foreign and domestic, wanted to

---

73. James Quinn, "GM: It's Rise, Fall and Future, *The Telegraph,* May 31, 2009, http://www.telegraph.co.uk/finance/newsbysector/transport/general-motors/5416646/GM-Its-rise-fall-and-future.html.

74. James M. Rubenstein, "Changing Distribution of the American Automobile Industry," *Geographical Review* 76, no. 3 (July 1986): 288–300.

avoid areas with large concentrations of unionized workers.[75] Japan's just-in-time (JIT) inventory process was spreading to the United States in the 1970s and '80s, and it required workers to be flexible and reliable. Asian manufacturers in the United States were concerned that union workers would be unwilling or unable to adapt to the JIT process they had created to keep inventory costs down.[76] The strife between unions and management that pervaded the US auto industry at the time also made management reluctant to locate new factories in areas where the new workforce would be influenced by existing union workers. Management believed workers in more rural areas that were relatively free of union influence would be less likely to engage in costly strikes. Japanese firms also believed that rural workers had a better work ethic than urban workers and thus were less likely to miss work and disrupt production.

The worker flexibility required by JIT also made locations outside of the Midwest more attractive. States with right-to-work laws, which prohibit compulsory union membership as a condition of employment, tend to have lower unionization rates. At the time, all the southern states had right-to-work laws, and this made them attractive alternatives to the midwestern states that lacked such laws. There's evidence that GM chose Tennessee as the location for its new Saturn plant due to it being the right-to-work state closest to its Michigan headquarters.[77] The US plants of foreign auto manufacturers also located in relatively rural locations and were often not unionized. Like GM's Saturn, Nissan chose Tennessee as the location of its first US assembly plant, which began production in 1983.

Despite higher unionization rates, the Midwest still had some advantages, such as its dense supplier networks that had built up over decades. Because of these advantages, many Asian manufacturers chose to locate in the region but outside of traditional urban locations where labor unions were concentrated. Honda, for example, chose Marysville, Ohio, located 33 miles northwest of Columbus, as the site of its first US plant, which opened in 1982.

In addition to greater worker flexibility, Asian companies also demanded higher-quality work. When some US suppliers were unwilling to adapt their production processes to meet the quality standards of Mazda and other Asian companies, the manufacturers were forced to invest in their own sup-

---

75. Rubenstein, "Changing Distribution," 298.

76. Andrew Mair, Richard Florida, and Martin Kenney, "The New Geography of Automobile Production: Japanese Transplants in North America," *Economic Geography* 64, no. 4 (1988): 352–73.

77. Rubenstein, "Changing Distribution," 299.

plier factories.[78] Since the use of JIT requires suppliers and assembly plants to be strategically located in proximity to one another, this also influenced the movement of automobile-related manufacturing out of dense metro areas and into more rural areas.

The rise of Japanese firms on US soil during the 1980s coincided with the relationship between management and labor unions becoming more amicable. The number of large strikes declined from several hundred per year to less than 50 annually on average. One watershed event that researchers and participants alike say contributed to the change in labor relations was President Ronald Reagan's 1981 decision to fire the striking unionized air traffic controllers.[79] After this event, companies began hiring permanent replacement workers more frequently in response to strikes, and this contributed to the decline in union power. The increased foreign competition also incentivized unions and management to work together to avoid being driven out of business. Instead of fighting each other, each group recognized that it was in its best interest to modernize and facilitate productivity growth in order survive in a world of increasing global competition.

Despite the improved relations between unions and firms, the shift of automakers from urban, union-concentrated areas to more rural, business-friendly areas never really reversed. The major automobile-related factories in Dayton's city limits shut down and many have since been razed or repurposed. For example, a former Delco factory building on First Street was converted to apartments in 2017, while the city's minor league baseball stadium, Fifth Third Field, was built nearby on the site of another Delco plant.

The last GM-related plant in the Dayton area was GM's Moraine Assembly Plant, where I worked one summer producing the Chevy Trailblazer, Oldsmobile Bravada, and GMC Envoy. Located just south of Dayton's city limits, the plant produced vehicles until 2008. It employed 2,400 workers when it closed that year. At the same time GM employed about 73,000 workers total, down from over 600,000 in the late 1970s. Also in 2008, GM lost its position as the best-selling car manufacturer to Toyota. In 2014, with the help of $9.7 million of tax subsidies from state and local government, the Moraine plant was purchased by Fuyao Glass America and today produces car windshields.[80]

---

78. Mair, Florida, and Kenney, "New Geography," 365.

79. Alder, Lagakos, and Ohanian, "Labor Market," 16.

80. "These 25 Projects Landed the Biggest Tax Credits," *Dayton Business Journal*, October 20, 2017, https://www.bizjournals.com/dayton/news/2017/10/20/these-25projects-landed-the-biggest-tax-credits.html#g/422463/26.

Earlier we discussed within-industry knowledge spillovers. Such knowledge spillovers, an example of localization economies, are the benefits that firms in the same industry receive when they locate near one another. The early work of Charles Kettering and Edward Deeds helped create a cluster of automobile-related manufacturing in Dayton and the surrounding metro area that was reinforced by localization economies: Firms shared ideas, suppliers, and distribution networks, and they could also draw from a large pool of workers comfortable and familiar with manufacturing employment. But as foreign competition increased and the US economy transitioned from a manufacturing economy to a service economy, these localization economies became less important. Eventually, the benefits of being clustered in and around Dayton weren't strong enough to overcome the costs, and employers relocated to more advantageous areas or shut down completely.

The economic decline of the entire Rust Belt, not just Dayton, coincides with an intense period of union-management conflict. Prior to 1980, the hold-up problem stifled investment in firms located in the Rust Belt and reduced productivity gains relative to other parts of the country. As a result, economic activity shifted to other regions of America. One study estimates that the combination of the hold-up problem and the decline in the costs of international trade that exposed American companies to foreign competition can explain over half of the decline in the Rust Belt's share of manufacturing employment from 1950 to 2000, with the hold-up problem explaining the bulk of it.[81] The decline was especially large from 1950 to 1980, when union power was the strongest, and then tapered off in the mid-1980s as union power weakened and productivity growth in the Rust Belt began to increase. This productivity growth improved the region's competitiveness and helped stabilize the region's local economies, but cities like Dayton have never completely recovered.

However, even in declining areas there are pockets of success. In his seminal work on cities and the job creation process, David Birch emphasized that every city loses jobs, but that successful cities are able to replace them.[82] Using data from 1969 to 1976 for ten metropolitan areas, Birch analyzed four different firm-level job flows: births, expansions, deaths, and contractions. He found that firm deaths and contractions occurred in all the cities at nearly the same rate, but that successful, growing cities had births and expansions that exceeded deaths and contractions. This led him to conclude

---

81. Alder, Lagakos, and Ohanian, "Labor Market."

82. David L. Birch, *Job Creation in Cities* (Cambridge, MA: MIT Program on Neighborhood and Regional Change, 1980).

that what matters for job growth, and thus population growth, at the city level is how well cities can replace jobs, which he called the "job replacement rate."

From 1972 to 1976, Birch found that Dayton's deaths and contraction rate was 8.4%, while the same rate in its suburbs was 6.6%. However, the suburbs replacement rate was 11% while Dayton's was only 6.8%.[83] Dayton's decline over this period and throughout the latter half of the twentieth century was not simply due to firms failing or contracting. Instead, it was due to the inability of Dayton's residents to replace firms and jobs as fast as they lost them. This is worth emphasizing: Cities aren't successful because they never lose jobs but because employment gains due to new business formations and expansions outpace employment losses from business failures and contractions. This implies that Dayton officials should focus less on saving or retaining jobs and more on improving the city's business environment so that it's easier for entrepreneurs to start and expand businesses. It's a city's ability to adapt to changing economic circumstances that leads to long-term success, and this is a topic we will return to later.

Crime in Dayton

Another factor commonly believed to be working against Dayton and other large cities since at least the early 1960s is crime. People don't want to live in places where they feel unsafe, and cities typically have higher crime rates than suburban and rural areas. Starting in the early 1960s, both violent and property crime rose across America. In 1960 the national violent crime rate was 161 crimes per 100,000 people. At its peak in the early 1990s it had risen nearly five-fold to 758. The national property crime rate followed a similar path, increasing from 1,726 crimes per 100,000 people to 5,140.[84] Since then the rates of both types of crime have declined, but they're still higher today than in 1960.

During the period of rising crime from 1960 to the early 1990s, many people attributed urban flight to the spike in crime. In *National Review* in 1994, economist Walter Williams wrote, "Today's crime rate, unimaginable a mere three or four decades ago, is driving cities into middle-class flight

83. Samuel Staley. Enterprise Zones and Inner City Economic Development: An Analysis of Firms in the Dayton, Ohio Enterprise Zone Program. Center for Urban and Public Affairs (1989), Wright State University.

84. The property crime rate actually peaked in 1980 before declining slightly during the mid-1980s and then rising again through the early 1990s.

(both black and white), bankruptcy, and economic waste."[85] And from the cover story of the July 11, 1977, issue of *Time* magazine:

> The ripple effects of crime eventually overwhelm a city and destroy its élan. People are frightened away from downtown, reducing business for stores, theaters, restaurants. In their place, thick as weeds, sprout porno houses, massage parlors and gambling havens, where criminals thrive.[86]

These casual observations about the effects of crime on the populations of cities are supported by more rigorous research. One study that analyzes data from 1970 to 1990 finds that a 10% increase in crime resulted in a 1% decline in a city's population on average over this period.[87] This might not sound like much of an effect, but remember that at the national level total crime (violent plus property) increased by around 200% between 1960 and 1990. Using the findings from the study, a similar increase at the city level would result in a 20% decline in the population of that city. The authors also find that adults with more than a high school education and who are parents were more likely to leave cities in response to an increase in crime than less-educated adults without children. This means that crime not only contributed to Dayton's population decline but also to the changing composition of the city since families with educated parents were more likely to leave than others.

Other studies are less conclusive about the effects of crime on people's decisions to move, but even these studies find that crime did impact where people located after they decided to move.[88] That is, once a person or family decided to move for a reason other than crime (perhaps to live in a better school district or a bigger house), the different crime rates between cities and suburbs influenced their decision about where to move to, with the lower-crime suburbs being the preferred destination.

Of course, changes in crime will only affect where people live if some places experience larger changes than others. If crime increases everywhere equally, there's no incentive to move. We can examine changes in crime in

85. Walter Williams, "Blacks, Jews, Liberals and Crime: Is the Black-Crime Problem a Crime Problem, or Is It a Poverty Problem, or an Education Problem?" *National Review*, May 16, 1994, 42.

86. "The Youth Crime Plague," *Time*, July 11, 1977, 20.

87. Julie Berry Cullen and Steven D. Levitt, "Crime, Urban Flight, and the Consequences for Cities," Review of Economics and Statistics 81, no. 2 (May 1999): 159–69.

88. Ingrid Gould Ellen and Katherine O'Regan, "Crime and Urban Flight Revisited: The Effect of the 1990s Drop in Crime on Cities," *Journal of Urban Economics* 68, no. 3 (2010): 247–59; Frey, "Central City White Flight."

Dayton and surrounding cities using the FBI's Uniform Crime Reporting Statistics database, which contains yearly crime data for local police agencies since 1985.[89] The total crime rate data—violent crimes plus property crimes per 100,000 people—for Dayton, Kettering, Huber Heights, Fairborn, Beavercreek, and Centerville are displayed in figure 5. The dots in figure 5 mark the year crime rates peaked in each city.

The crime-rate gap between Dayton and its suburbs increased from 1985 to 1989. Over this period, Dayton's total crime rate increased by 25%. Meanwhile, Fairborn's rate increased by 21%, Kettering and Centerville's by about 15%, and Beavercreek's by only 2%. Huber Heights's data doesn't start until 1989 so the change for this period can't be calculated. The different changes in crime rates mean Dayton became relatively more dangerous than its surrounding suburbs in the late 1980s—a phenomenon that occurred in cities across America—and this can help explain the 6% decline in Dayton's population from 1980 to 1990.

Crime rates in Dayton, Kettering, and Centerville all peaked in 1989, while the rates in the other three suburbs peaked ten or more years later. The later peaks in Huber Heights, Beavercreek, and Fairborn are part of a narrowing crime-rate gap between Dayton and its suburbs since Dayton's 1989 peak. That is, Dayton has become relatively safer since the 1990s. Yet despite this narrowing crime gap, Dayton's crime rate remains about two to three times higher than the suburban rates.

While there is evidence that the increase in crime after 1960 led to a decrease in the population of Dayton and other cities, the subsequent decline in crime starting in the early 1990s did not lead to a similar increase in city populations. As shown in figure 5, the crime rate in Dayton fell by nearly 50% from 1989 to 2014, and the gap between it and the rates of its suburbs narrowed considerably. Yet despite becoming relatively safer, Dayton's population declined by an additional 40,000 people over this period.

Other things occurred as crime was declining in the 1990s, so it could be that those factors—declining employment opportunities in cities, rising incomes that increased demand for bigger suburban homes, or something else—overwhelmed any effect from falling crime. But even when researchers control for these other factors, it still doesn't appear that the decline in city crime rates caused people to repopulate cities.[90] However, there is evidence that the decline in crime slowed migration from central cities to the suburbs.

---

89. Uniform Crime Reporting Statistics, US Department of Justice, last revised January 26, 2017, https://www.ucrdatatool.gov/Search/Crime/Crime.cfm.

90. Ellen and O'Regan, "Crime and Urban Flight," 247–59.

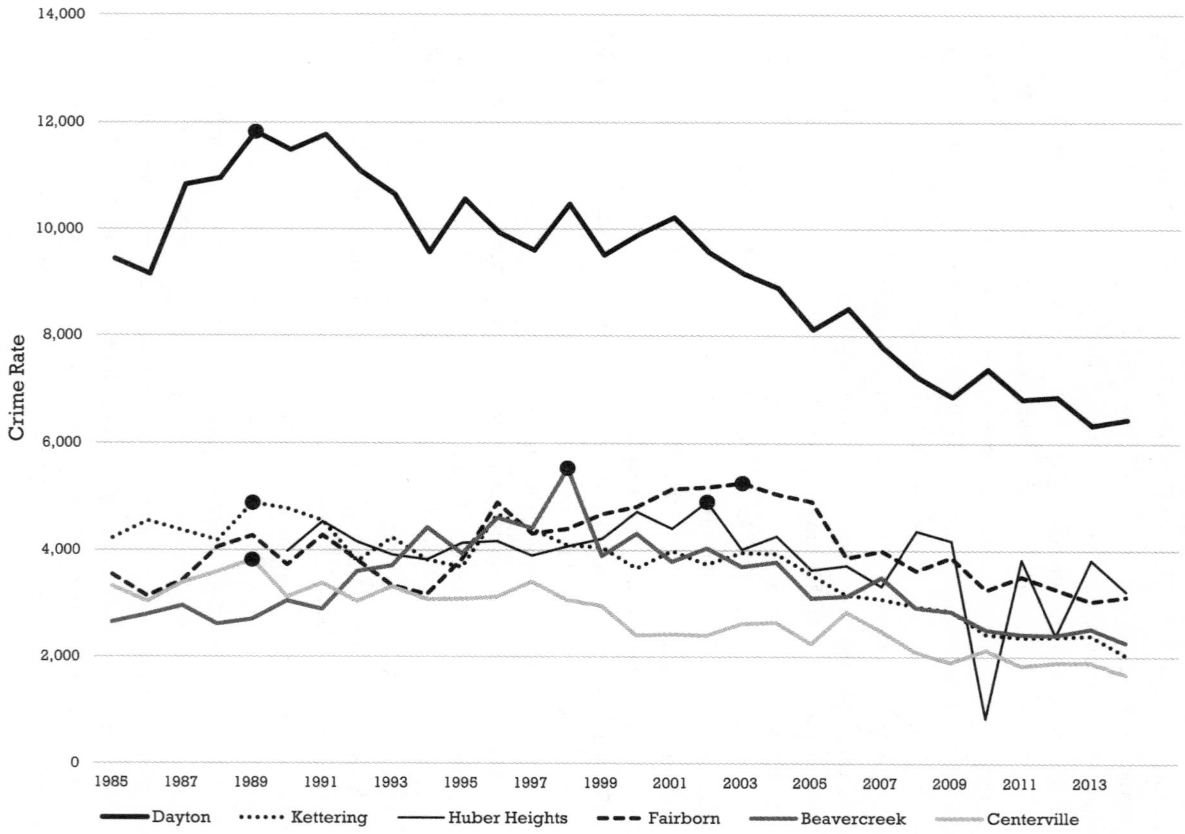

FIGURE 5. Total crime rate in Dayton area cities, 1985–2014

It's safe to say that increases in crime certainly don't improve the quality of life in cities, and, all things considered, it appears such increases played a modest role in people—especially families with educated parents—leaving cities for the suburbs. The later decline in crime that occurred in the 1990s and through the 2000s reduced migration to the suburbs but didn't reverse it.

Economist Albert Hirschman wrote an influential book, *Exit, Voice, and Loyalty*, which helps explain why the more recent decline in crime hasn't led to a big increase in population in cities like Dayton.[91] We touched on Hirschman's ideas about exit and voice in our earlier discussion about local election turnout (voice) and migration (exit) in Dayton in the 1950s. In his book, Hirschman presents a theory of how people express dissatisfaction to firms and other organizations after a decline in product or service quality. For a city, exit is demonstrated by migration: Dissatisfied residents migrate to a community that better matches their preferences for local government services and fiscal policy. Voice, on the other hand, requires staying in place, and in cities it is usually manifested through voting. Other forms of voice in regard to cities are protests, letters, phone calls, and public comments directed at officials.

Hirschman explains that loyalty plays a role in whether someone expresses dissatisfaction with voice or exit. Someone who is loyal to a city will be less likely to exit due to a given deterioration in quality. In this way, loyalty limits the use of exit and stimulates the use of voice. If exit is too easy, the quality-conscious people most capable of using voice to elicit change— people with higher incomes and more education, for example—will tend to leave early. The loss of these people can generate further deterioration that causes more people to leave.

However, if some of the most quality-conscious residents are loyal they will remain in place, at least initially, and try to fix a city's problems from within—that is, they will use some method of voice. According to Hirschman, loyalty can be conscious or unconscious. Conscious loyalty means that the loyal residents are aware of the quality decline and decide to stay to try to improve the situation. Unconscious loyalty means that residents stay without realizing that quality is deteriorating. This could occur because the decline doesn't start at the same time in every neighborhood or because people believe the decline is temporary.

The presence of loyalty implies that cities will initially lose people slowly as their quality deteriorates. Consciously loyal residents will stick around

---

91. Albert O. Hirschman, Exit, Voice, and Loyalty: Responses to Decline in Firms, Organizations, and States (Cambridge, MA: Harvard University Press, 1970), 90.

and partake in efforts to get the city back on track. Only if they are unable to turn things around and the city's quality continues to decline will they leave. And if the decline continues, the unconsciously loyal will eventually notice it or they'll realize that it's not temporary and they will leave. Loyalty can initially temper migration away from the city, but if quality continues to decline migration will speed up as even the most loyal decide to exit.

The pattern of initially low migration followed by higher migration once loyalty is exhausted is repeated as a city recovers. Only in this case, an initial quality improvement induces a relatively small amount of migration back to the city. It will take a large, sustained improvement in quality to generate significant population growth since most people will need confirmation that the city has improved and will continue to do so before they will return.

What is interesting about this analysis is that it generates two different populations, one low and one high, for the same level of quality. If Hirschman's model is correct, then even if the crime rate in Dayton in 2000 returned to its 1980 level, we shouldn't expect a population increase similar in size to the population decrease that occurred from 1980 to 1990. Hirschman's model applies to declines in city quality other than a crime increase, such as a decline in city service quality, fewer job opportunities, or inefficient tax policy. To reverse widespread decline and population loss, Dayton and cities like it will have to make substantial, long-lasting quality improvements.

Even though the studies that examine crime and city population growth in the 1990s don't find much of an effect from falling crime rates, that doesn't mean there was no effect in every city. The results of large-scale empirical work are average effects and they can hide individual successes and failures. Dayton's population, along with the populations of most other midwestern and northeastern cities, continued to fall in the 1990s, despite becoming relatively safer.[92] But the populations of three cold-weather central cities—New York, Chicago, and Boston—grew in the 1990s along with the decline in urban crime. But in addition to growing populations and falling crime rates, these cities had another important thing in common: populations with a lot of human capital, which as we have seen is a big predictor of city growth. These three cold-weather cities were able to grow along with the decline in crime because their skilled workforces enabled them to reinvent themselves.

---

92. Edward L. Glaeser and Jesse M. Shapiro, "Urban Growth in the 1990s: Is City Living Back?," *Journal of Regional Science* 43, no. 1 (2003): 139–65.

Dayton's Decline Summarized

Now that we have discussed the big causes of urban decline in Dayton and the Rust Belt more broadly—white flight, the interstate highway system, the hold-up problem and lack of innovation/human capital, and crime—we can construct a timeline of the causes of decline in Dayton.

Previously we saw that Dayton's white population began declining in the 1950s (see figure 3). Meanwhile, the suburbs surrounding the city—Kettering, Beavercreek, Fairborn, Vandalia, etc.—were growing rapidly. Poorer, less-educated blacks had moved north in large numbers for several decades by the 1950s, and many had moved to Dayton to find work, particularly in the 1940s when demand for labor in Dayton was high due to World War II production. These facts are consistent with the story of white flight due to racial prejudice or an aversion to low-income southern migrants. The timing also shows that highways were not necessary for urban white flight. The interstates running through and around Dayton—I-75 and I-675—were not completed until the mid-1960s and mid-1980s. In the case of Dayton, it doesn't appear that the interstate system initiated the city's decline.

That said, the decline of the city's white population accelerated over the next two decades: From 1960 to 1980 the white population fell by over 85,000, a 42% decline. This was much larger than the 5,000 persons or 2.2% decline from 1950 to 1960. The completion of I-75 in the mid-1960s made it easier for many suburban residents to commute to Dayton for work and likely contributed to the accelerated departure of higher-income whites to the suburbs. Dayton's black population, on the other hand, continued to grow and didn't peak until 1980, 30 years after the white population's peak.

The job losses of the 1970s and early '80s further exacerbated Dayton's decline. Many of the city's factories closed, in part due to the hold-up problem that hindered innovation and productivity growth. Many other employers who survived eventually moved to the suburbs where space was cheaper and the commuting costs of their suburban employees were lower. For example, Reynolds and Reynolds, a software and professional services supplier to automobile dealers founded in Dayton in 1866, began moving its employees out of downtown Dayton after it broke ground on a new Kettering headquarters in 1997. Today, all its approximately 1,300 Dayton-area employees work at the headquarters.[93]

---

93. "About Us," Reynolds and Reynolds, accessed January 26, 2018, http://www.reyrey.com/company/index.asp.

Like many other cities, Dayton's employment base depended on a hand-ful of large companies—NCR, GM—and when these employers downsized, left, or closed down, there was a dearth of innovative new companies to take their place due to the city's low human capital and subsequent lack of innovation. The employment losses encouraged further population decline: From 1980 to 2010, the city's total population declined from over 193,000 to 141,527. But unlike in previous decades, both whites and blacks left the city on net over this period. The white population declined by 45,000 people and was at just over 73,000 in 2010, while the black population declined by almost 15,000 people and settled at 60,700 the same year.

The remaining big factor that contributed to Dayton's population decline was crime. Crime rates increased in cities nationwide from the 1960s until the late-1980s, and research shows that this also contributed to declining urban populations. However, rising crime rates can also be a result of popu-lation decline, since fewer people—especially higher-income people—means less tax revenue, which tends to strain city resources and makes it harder to enforce the law. Public sector unions play a role in this due to their multi-year contracts and political influence, both of which make it harder for local governments to cut spending or reallocate resources as fast as population decline may warrant. We will further discuss this later when we examine Dayton's finances in the latter half of the twentieth century.

While crime likely contributed to Dayton's population decline, it is best thought of as a secondary cause that reinforced the decline that was already taking place. Even when the total crime rate in Dayton improved relative to the surrounding suburban cities beginning in the early 1990s, Dayton's population continued to shrink. This is an indication that crime was often not the deciding factor in people's decisions to leave Dayton and settle in the suburbs.

Finally, we should not forget about the role of climate and geography. Even without southerners migrating northward, the interstate highway sys-tem, the hold-up problem, and rising crime rates, many people would have eventually left the Midwest and Northeast for sunnier, more temperate cli-mates. Improvements in transportation, the spread of air conditioning, and the eradication of malaria improved the attractiveness of southern and west-ern states relative to the northern states over the course of the twentieth century, and people responded by moving. Sunny days and mild winters are also normal goods, meaning people demand more of them as incomes increase, so as Americans got richer areas with those amenities became more popular. The Sun Belt provides some natural advantages that midwestern cities like Dayton can't match, and many people will continue to move to take advantage of them.

Based on this analysis, the story of Dayton's population decline can be summarized as follows: White flight from the city in response to southern migration was later facilitated by highways, which made it cheaper to live in the suburbs and commute to Dayton for work. As the city's population declined, houses sat vacant, crime increased, and some companies relocated to other cities or suburban locations to be closer to their workforces. Other companies shut down due to competition from more productive firms, both foreign and domestic, and were not replaced. The high crime rate and lack of employment opportunities encouraged further migration of both blacks and whites out of Dayton in the last two decades of the twentieth century, and this has continued into the twenty-first century. All the while, incomes overall have been rising, which makes the Sun Belt more attractive, causing people to move south and west in pursuit of sunny days and mild winters.

The Aftermath

During the 1980s Dayton officials and business leaders began acknowledging that the economy was changing and attempted to adapt via top-down planning. After economic changes brought on by the recessions of the '70s and early '80s and the decline of the US automotive industry, local officials began making plans to leverage nearby Wright-Patterson Air Force Base to attract technology firms to a new high-tech research park located in the Dayton suburbs of Kettering and Beavercreek.[94] The park contains 1,250 acres of land, but only about 450 acres have been developed since 1984. Also, one of the big companies that located there is the aforementioned Reynolds and Reynolds, which is not a net gain to the metro area since it relocated from Dayton. Ultimately, the park has failed to deliver the anticipated economic activity to the metro area and has even proven to be bad for Dayton since it provided an opportunity for firms such as Reynolds and Reynolds to relocate outside Dayton's city limits.

Then, in 2009, Dayton's flagship company NCR—its last Fortune 500 Company, the company founded by Dayton native John H. Patterson, and the company that rescued Dayton from the 1913 flood—relocated to the

---

94. Lynn Wasnak, "Dayton: A City of the Future," Ohio Business 9, no. 1 (September 1985: 41–47.

Atlanta metro area. This further harmed Dayton's economy, but perhaps the most damaging effect was to Dayton's psyche.[95] In many ways it symbolized the end of Dayton as an economically important midwestern city.

Luckily, the story doesn't end there. In 2009 the University of Dayton purchased NCR's former Dayton headquarters. The 115-acre site was named UD's "River Campus." The university used the 455,000-square-foot building to house the University of Dayton Research Institute, which was founded in 1956, as well as the university's alumni center, some graduate classes, and conference space.[96] From an urban growth standpoint, it's encouraging to see the space occupied by a university that is expanding its graduate programs and research capabilities, both of which should increase the city's human capital and skill levels in the long run, while also contributing to a culture of innovation. The Research Institute focuses on practical science and engineering solutions to real-world problems, and to the extent it's successful it should help Dayton and the entire metro area. No solitary institute or group of researchers can single-handedly revitalize Dayton, but this repurposing of NCR's former headquarters is a step in the right direction that should help cushion the blow of losing a company as significant as NCR.

There are other reasons to be optimistic as well. Of the major causes of decline discussed here—urban white flight, highway construction, uncompetitive labor markets, lack of an innovative workforce, and crime—most have improved in midwestern cities relative to other regions and the suburbs. Union power has declined in the Midwest, which has made the region and its cities more competitive. And the nationwide shift from a manufacturing economy to a service-sector/knowledge economy means that dense cities that facilitate the spread of information should have a productivity advantage over less dense areas for the foreseeable future.

Furthermore, new highway construction is practically over and it's not clear there's enough funding available to increase capacity or even maintain the current system. If nothing changes, this means more congestion and longer commutes from the suburbs in many metro areas, which should increase the attractiveness of central cities as places to live. Crime has also fallen in cities relative to their suburbs, as we showed with Dayton, which should make cities more attractive. Finally, people have generally become more tolerant of one another since the 1960s and 70s, especially younger

95. Dan Barry, "In a Company's Hometown, the Emptiness Echoes," *New York Times*, January 24, 2010, http://www.nytimes.com/2010/01/25/us/25land.html?_r=0.

96. University of Dayton, "University Buys NCR Headquarters," news release, December 21, 2009, https://udayton.edu/news/articles/2009/university_buys_ncr_headquarters.php.

generations.[97] Thus, the racial and lower-income prejudices that contributed to people leaving cities for the suburbs are less of a factor today than in the past. All these occurrences are a good sign for Dayton and other cities going forward.

How Other Ohio Cities Have Fared and Lessons for Dayton

It's important to note that Dayton is not the only Ohio city to experience population decline over the last few decades. Figure 6 shows the populations of Ohio's six largest cities from 1980 to 2010 (measured on the left vertical axis) and the population of Ohio over the same period (measured on the right vertical axis).

Columbus is the only major city in Ohio that has gained population since 1980 even though the state of Ohio grew by 7% from 1980 to 2010. The other five cities—Cleveland, Cincinnati, Toledo, Akron, and Dayton—experienced steady population decline over this period.

The population numbers slightly improve at the metro area level. Both the Columbus and Cincinnati metro areas grew by several hundred thousand people from 1980 to 2010, while the metro area populations in Dayton, Cleveland, Toledo, and Akron declined only slightly or were relatively constant.[98] Today the Cincinnati metro area is the state's largest (2.17 million people), followed by Cleveland (2.05 million) and then Columbus (2.04 million). Interestingly, the Dayton metro area is the fourth largest in Ohio, at around 800,000 people, despite having the smallest central city of the group.

Among the cities losing population from 1980 to 2010, the Cincinnati metro area is still attracting people, even if they do not end up in the city limits of Cincinnati. This can still help Cincinnati if it is able to attract suburban consumers to the downtown area. One of the strategies of modern urban revitalization is turning downtowns into places where people go to eat, shop, socialize over beers or coffee, enjoy concerts and performances, and attend festivals. Cities that are no longer places of production because of job losses may become places of consumption, referred to as consumer

97. John Wihbey, "White Racial Attitudes over Time: Data from the General Social Survey," updated August 14, 2014, https://journalistsresource.org/studies/society/race-society/white-racial-attitudes-over-time-data-general-social-survey.

98. Bureau of Economic Analysis, Local Area Personal Income and Employment data, Economic Profile Table CA30.

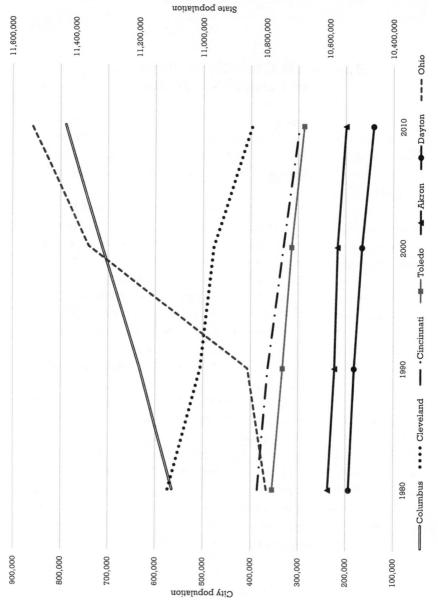

FIGURE 6. Ohio city populations, 1980–2010. (Data from https://www.citypopulation.de/USA-Ohio.html.)

cities.[99] A growing metro area provides a large customer base for a central consumer city, which is a strategy that may work in Cincinnati.

However, government efforts to artificially create consumer-driven downtowns often fail to produce lasting results despite costing taxpayers millions of dollars. There is little evidence that economic incentive programs designed to increase employment or generate economic development more broadly succeed. Several studies find that tax breaks for specific companies or tax breaks that are only available to firms in specific neighborhoods have no effect on total investment or employment growth in a city, while some even find a negative effect.[100] Even in studies that find a positive effect, it is usually quite small.[101]

Regarding Ohio in particular, researcher Benjamin Clark finds that there is little evidence that economic incentive programs in Ohio have resulted in any meaningful economic development.[102] In an overview of the state tax incentives literature, researcher Terry Buss notes that many studies yield conflicting results and thus provide little guidance to policy makers about what programs or incentives, if any, actually work.[103]

City officials also often support large conspicuous projects like new sports stadiums to act as an anchor for additional development, but such large-scale projects rarely achieve their goal. In fact, one study finds a possible negative impact on local economic development from the subsidization of sports stadiums.[104] In a summary of the relevant research on the economic

99. Edward L. Glaeser, Jed Kolko, and Albert Saiz, "Consumer City," *Journal of Economic Geography* 1, no. 1 (2001): 27–50.

100. William F. Fox and Matthew N. Murray, "Do Economic Effects Justify the Use of Fiscal Incentives?," *Southern Economic Journal* 71, no. 1 (July 2004): 78–92; Alan Peters and Peter Fisher, "The Failures of Economic Development Incentives," *Journal of the American Planning Association* 70, no. 1 (Winter 2004): 27–37; Michael D. LaFaive and Michael J. Hicks, "*MEGA: A Retrospective Assessment*" (Mackinac Center for Public Policy, 2005); Todd M. Gabe and David S. Kraybill, "The Effect of State Economic Development Incentives on Employment Growth of Establishments," *Journal of Regional Science* 42, no. 4 (2002): 703–30.

101. Dagney Faulk, "Do State Economic Development Incentives Create Jobs? An Analysis of State Employment Tax Credits," *National Tax Journal* 55, no. 2 (June 2002): 263–80.

102. Benjamin Y. Clark, "Can Tax Expenditures Stimulate Growth in Rust Belt Cities?," in *The Road through the Rust Belt: From Preeminence to Decline to Prosperity*, ed. William M. Bowen (Kalamazoo, MI: Upjohn Institute for Employment Research, 2014): 37–68.

103. Terry F. Buss, "The Effect of State Tax Incentives on Economic Growth and Firm Location Decisions: An overview of the Literature," *Economic Development Quarterly* 15, no. 1 (February 2001): 90–105.

104. Robert A. Baade and Richard F. Dye, "The Impact of Stadium and Professional Sports on Metropolitan Area Development," *Growth and Change* 21, no. 2 (1990): 1–14.

effects of sports teams, the authors find "virtually no evidence of economic development benefits from sports teams or stadiums."[105] Additionally, economist Dennis Coates finds some evidence that sports teams may actually hurt economic growth.[106]

When it comes to stadiums or other large projects like convention centers, city officials need to keep in mind that such projects take up a lot of land that could be used for other more productive things. Many people believe that sports stadiums generate urban development because they focus on what is seen rather than what could have been. It's easy to see the people who attend the games and nearby restaurants and bars during the sport's season. But this ignores the opportunity cost of the stadium—that is, what would have existed had the stadium never been built. While sports teams are not bad in and of themselves, the evidence doesn't support the idea that sports teams provide an economic benefit to the surrounding area.

Despite the robust empirical evidence that sports teams don't do much to improve urban economies, Dayton officials pursued this consumer-driven, sports stadium strategy in the late 1990s. The result was Fifth Third Field, home of the Class-A Dayton Dragons baseball team, which opened in the city's downtown in 2000. While there has been some new development in the area immediately surrounding the stadium, it has largely failed to revitalize the city's broader downtown and, as we have seen, it has not stemmed the city's population loss. This outcome is consistent with the research discussed previously and a more recent study of minor league baseball stadiums that includes Firth Third Field as one of the observations.[107] This study finds some evidence that minor league stadiums help the neighborhoods in proximity to them, but only because these neighborhoods absorb new development at the expense of other neighborhoods that are farther away. Stadiums concentrate economic development but they don't create citywide economic growth.

Meanwhile, Dayton spent about $23 million to help construct the stadium, including an $11 million loan whose principle declines each year the team remains in Dayton.[108] The loan will be fully forgiven after the team's

105. John Siegfried and Andrew Zimbalist, "The Economics of Sports Facilities and Their Communities," *Journal of Economic Perspectives* 14, no. 3 (Summer 2000): 95–114.

106. Dennis Coates, "Growth Effects of Sports Franchises, Stadiums, and Arenas: 15 Years Later," Mercatus Working Paper (2015).

107. Eric Joseph van Holm, "Minor Stadiums, Major Effects? Patterns and Sources of Redevelopment Surrounding Minor League Baseball Stadiums," *Urban Studies* (April 26, 2018): 672–88.

108. Julian March, "How Other Cities Have Funded Baseball Stadiums," StarNews, October 19, 2012, http://www.starnewsonline.com/news/20121019/how-other-cities-have-funded-baseball-stadiums.

twentieth season, essentially making it a grant rather than a loan. City officials and many residents seem to enjoy having the Dragons in town, but the research implies that the $23 million in taxpayer money didn't provide a net benefit to the city.

Dayton's population decline began in the 1960s and hasn't let up since, despite common urban revitalization efforts such as subsidized sports stadiums. Meanwhile, the metro area's population has remained relatively constant over the last 30 years at around 800,000 people, in part because many of the people who left Dayton settled in the surrounding suburbs. Population decline often puts pressure on a city's finances, and the financial decisions cities make in response to this pressure can exacerbate their decline. In the next chapter we examine Dayton's finances over the latter half of the twentieth century and discuss Dayton's public-sector unions.

CHAPTER 5

Dayton's Finances and Public-Sector Unions

T   **HE PREVIOUS** chapter discussed the major causes of Dayton's population and economic decline that began in the 1960s: urban white flight, highway construction, a lack of human capital, declining innovation among firms, and crime. All these things encouraged high-skill workers to leave the city or, if they were new to the area, to locate in one of the newer and growing suburbs. This reduced the skill level of the city's workforce and made it difficult for the city to reinvent itself in response to increasing global competition and other economic changes. Now we will look at Dayton's finances to see how the economic and demographic changes that took place in the latter half of the twentieth century impacted the financial health of the city.

Our examination of Dayton's finances begins in 1951. Total expenditures increased dramatically in inflation-adjusted dollars from 1951 to 2006, rising from $106 million to $386 million, a 264% increase.[1] And remember, this increase occurred even though Dayton's population was declining.

---

1. US Census Bureau, Annual Survey of Local Government Finances and Census of Governments (1951–2006). As stated in the documentation, "the data presented here are statistical in nature and do not represent an accounting statement. A difference between total revenue and expenditure does not necessarily indicate a 'budget' surplus or deficit." Still, the data are useful for highlighting long-term trends.

Despite the decline in population, tax revenue mostly kept pace with expenditures. Between 1951 and 1984 Dayton ran a fairly balanced budget. Some years it had a surplus and in other years a deficit, but this is to be expected since budgeting relies on forecasts made with imperfect information.[2] The only period of sustained and significant deficits was from 1988 to 1994. Once these deficits subsided, total revenue and expenditure growth slowed significantly, meaning that practically all the aforementioned 264% increase occurred between 1951 and 1994.[3]

Economist William Baumol attributes the rising expenditures of a city government over time to what is known as the "cost disease."[4] The main symptom of the cost disease is a rising cost of government, in particular the cost of government-provided goods and services that are labor intensive. Figure 7 depicts the per capita cost of police protection, fire protection, and current expenditures for Dayton during select years from 1951 to 2006.[5] Current expenditures are total expenditures less capital outlays and are the amount of money spent by the government to operate on a daily basis and service previously accrued debt.

The per capita expenditures for all three categories increased from 1951 to 2000. From 2000 to 2006 all three measures declined slightly, which is consistent with the slowing growth of overall spending during this period. The largest increases occurred from 1960 to 1990, which is also when Dayton was experiencing its largest decline in population.

Why do the costs of government services rise as cities grow and often fail to decline as cities lose population? One explanation can be found in public choice theory, which is often summarized as politics without romance, meaning it treats politicians and government officials as just as self-interested as other people. In the public choice framework, politicians aren't impartial actors who only care about the public good. Most do care about the public good, at least as they define it, but they also want to win elections and stay in office. The desire to win elections leads them to seek out the support of people who can help them, even if the people who can help

2. See Richard E. Wagner, *Deficits, Debt, and Democracy: Wrestling with Tragedy on the Fiscal Commons* (Northampton, Massachusetts: Edward Elgar Publishing, 2012), 1.

3. US Census Bureau, Survey of Local Governments (1951–2006).

4. William J. Baumol, "Macroeconomics of Unbalanced Growth: The Anatomy of Urban Crisis," *The American Economic Review* 57, no. 3 (June 1967): 415–26.

5. Due to the limited availability of accurate historical city population data, only decennial census years are depicted prior to 2000. 1950 population data was used for the 1951 calculations.

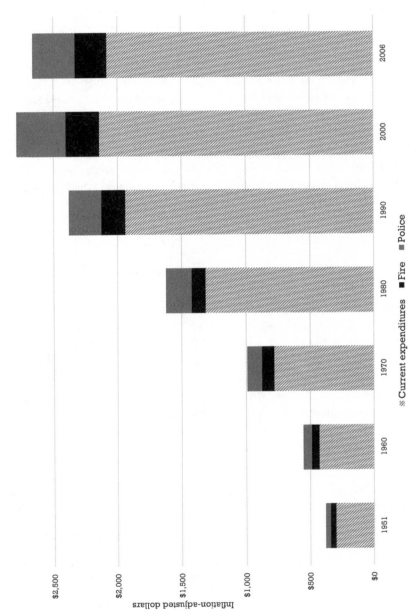

FIGURE 7. Dayton per capita expenditures, 1951–2006. US Census Bureau, Annual Survey of Local Government Finances and Census of Governments (1951–2006). Adjusted for inflation to 2009 dollars.

them have some interests that conflict with other voters and taxpayers. At the local level, public sector unions sometimes play this role.

Public sector unions want to raise the wages and protect the jobs of their members, which is understandably the primary goal of any union. Many of the public-sector industries—policing, firefighting, education, etc.—have high rates of unionization and unions tend to resist technology that increases productivity because it also reduces costs by eliminating positions. Thus, the political clout of unions and their desire to protect their members, combined with politicians' desire to win elections, often make it difficult for cities to control costs. Public-sector unions also partially institutionalize steady wage increases and stable or increasing employment levels through their monopoly power—cities must use the union for their labor needs—which helps explain why per capita costs increase even as population declines. All of this suggests that one way to relieve municipalities of the cost disease is the privatization of some city services.[6]

Public-Sector Unions in Dayton

There is substantial evidence that public-sector unionization leads to higher wages and higher nonwage benefits such as generous retirement plans, which increase the cost of providing local government goods and services.[7] One study finds that the presence of a union bargaining unit within a city department, such as sanitation or fire, significantly increases pay and total spending on that department.[8] Higher compensation for union workers is often attributed to their political clout, and another study supports this notion by finding that an increase in union political activity leads to higher compensation for public employee union members.[9] Cities that do not have a unionized workforce are not required to purchase labor from only one

6. J. Stephen Ferris and Edwin G. West, "The Cost Disease and Government Growth: Qualifications to Baumol," *Public Choice* 89 no. 1–2 (1996): 35–52.

7. For a study of police unions, see Ann Bartel and David Lewin, "Wages and Unionism in the Public Sector: The Case of Police," *The Review of Economics and Statistics* 63, no. 1 (February 1981): 53–59. For more general studies, see Jeffrey Zax and Casey Ichniowski, "The Effects of Public Sector Unionism on Pay, Employment, Department Budgets, and Municipal Expenditures," in *When Public Sector Workers Unionize, ed. Richard B. Freeman and Casey Ichniowski* (Chicago: University of Chicago Press, 1988), 323–64, and Chris Edwards, "Public Sector Unions and the Rising Costs of Employee Compensation," *Cato Journal* 30 (2010): 87.

8. Zax and Ichniowski, "Effects of Public Sector Unionism," 323–64.

9. Kevin M. O'Brien, "Compensation, Employment, and the Political Activity of Public Employee Unions," *Journal of Labor Research* 13 no. 2 (1992): 189–203.

provider, which makes it easier for them to provide government goods and services at a lower cost.

Dayton's city employees are unionized today, but that was not always the case.[10] In fact, if Dayton had followed state law, it would have avoided a unionized labor force until at least 1983, when Ohio finally enacted legislation allowing public sector collective bargaining.[11] Until 1983 local governments in Ohio were not allowed to enter into contracts with unions, a result that stemmed from a 1947 Ohio State Supreme Court case that declared municipal contracts with unions an improper delegation of authority. Also in 1947, the Ohio legislature enacted the Ferguson Act, which banned public employee strikes and enabled local governments to terminate strikers. In addition, rehired strikers would not get a pay increase for one year and were put on probation for two years.[12] Together, these bills not only made it easy for municipalities to avoid bargaining with public sector unions, they made it their legal duty.

These laws were rarely enforced, however, and the ruling that declared public sector bargaining an improper delegation of authority was the first to fall. Cincinnati formalized a relationship with the American Federation of State, County, and Municipal Employees (AFSCME) in 1960, and by 1968 Dayton, Cleveland, Columbus, and other major Ohio cities had also signed contracts with the AFSCME.[13] In 1975 the de facto acceptance of public sector bargaining was solidified in the Dayton-centric Ohio Supreme Court case *Dayton Classroom Teachers Association v. Dayton Board of Education*. In that case the court ruled that school boards had the authority to bargain with their employees and any contract reached would be enforceable in court.[14]

In the late 1960s several public-sector employee unions in Ohio went on strike, but the penalties of the Ferguson Act were seldom invoked.[15] Such strikes continued into the 1970s, and the consequences of a public employee strike became apparent in Dayton when the city's fire department went on

10. Dayton firefighters belong to the Ohio Association of Professional Fire Fighters Local 136, Dayton police officers belong to the Fraternal Order of Police of Ohio, and other Dayton public employees belong to the American Federation of State, County, and Municipal Employees Local 101.

11. Gregory M. Saltzman, "Public Sector Bargaining Laws Really Matter: Evidence from Ohio and Illinois" in *Freeman and Ichniowski, Public Sector Workers*, 41–80.

12. Saltzman, "Public Sector Bargaining," 41–80.

13. Saltzman, "Public Sector Bargaining," 41–80.

14. Saltzman, "Public Sector Bargaining," 41–80.

15. Saltzman, "Public Sector Bargaining," 41–80.

strike for three days in August 1977.[16] During the strike, it was reported that many residents were left to fight fires in their neighborhood with garden hoses.[17] In one such instance, children were credited with containing a fire until a neighboring municipal fire department arrived to take over. By the time the strike ended, more than 20 fires had broken out in the city and approximately 20 families lost their homes.[18] As a sign of the distrust this strike generated, there was even some suspicion that the striking firefighters had started some of the fires, though this claim was never substantiated. On the fourth day of the strike, the firefighters' union and the city finally agreed to a two-year contract that gave firefighters a $0.50 raise over the life of the contract and a shorter work week. Unsurprisingly, this event tarnished the national image of both the fire department and Dayton.[19]

Several comprehensive pro-union bills were introduced in the Ohio legislature from 1947 to 1982, but none of them garnered enough support to become law. That changed in 1982 when Democrats won control of both houses of the legislature and the governorship, and a comprehensive pro-union bill was finally enacted into law in 1983 without a single Republican vote.[20] This law was considered more pro-union than most public-sector statutes in other states and included provisions for binding interest arbitration for public safety employees (but prohibited strikes), mandatory dues checkoff, and authorized the agency shop, among other things.[21] This law had a negligible effect on Dayton since as stated previously the large cities in Ohio had already been engaging in collective bargaining for years.

Based on the evidence showing that unions increase municipal labor costs, Dayton officials' early acceptance of public sector collective bargaining likely contributed to the rising per capita costs between 1960 and 1990

---

16. UPI, "Dayton Firefighters OK Pact; Go to Work," *Chicago Tribune*, August 11, 1977, 1:14.

17. AP, "Dayton Residents Fighting Blazes as Firefighters Strike," *Hendersonville Times-News* August 10, 1977, 14, https://news.google.com/newspapers?nid=1665&dat=19770810&id=5D8aAAAAIBAJ&sjid=gyQEAAAAIBAJ&pg=6212,4007334&hl=en.

18. UPI, "Dayton Firefighters OK Pact," 1:14.

19. Editorial Board, "Dayton's Horrible Example," *Chicago Tribune*, August 13, 1977, 1:6, http://archives.chicagotribune.com/1977/08/13/page/6/article/daytons-horrible-example.

20. Saltzman, "Public Sector Bargaining," 41–80.

21. Saltzman, "Public Sector Bargaining," 41–80. Dues checkoff is the automatic withholding of union dues from an employee's paycheck. Under agency shop, all employees are required to pay some dues to the union covering their employment even if they are not members. Such an arrangement was ruled a violation of First Amendment rights in the 2018 US Supreme Court case *Janus v. American Federation of State, County, and Municipal Employees, Council 31*, No. 16-1466, 585 U.S.

shown in figure 7. The firefighters' union strike of 1977 also tarnished the city's image at a time when its population was already in decline. If Dayton would have abided by state law, it could have avoided the cost increase associated with unionization prior to the pro-union bill of 1983, at which time Dayton would have likely joined other municipalities in having a unionized workforce. That said, it's difficult to know the exact amount of the cost increase (in figure 7) that is due to Dayton's early acceptance of collective bargaining.

More recent data shows that Dayton's finances are in good shape compared to other cities. Between 2000 and 2016, Dayton's population declined by 15.4%, but most of this decline—14.7% of it—occurred between 2000 and 2010. Since 2010 Dayton's population has remained fairly stable, hovering around 140,000 people. The city's total revenues and total expenditures declined accordingly over this period.

Adjusted for inflation, Dayton's total revenue from 2002 to 2016 fell from $417 million to $314 million.[22] Per capita revenue fell from $2,569 to $2,237 over the same period, a 13% decline, which is about half of the 25% decline in total revenue. This shows that nearly half of the overall decline in total revenue from 2002 to 2016 was due to a declining population rather than declining revenue per person. That said, a 13% decline in per capita revenue is not trivial. Over this period, city officials cut expenditures accordingly and thus Dayton maintained a small surplus each year, but further declines in per capita revenue may make cutting expenditures more difficult, both politically and financially, which would put stress on Dayton's budget.

Despite the recent drop in revenue, Dayton's officials and residents have been relatively responsible compared to other midwestern and northeastern city dwellers, and this has allowed them to keep the city's long-term debt under control. According to data from the Manhattan Institute, Dayton has decreased the long-term debt burden of its residents over the last 40 years despite the city's shrinking population.[23] In 1972 Dayton's long-term debt burden was $1,373 per person. By 2015 it had fallen to $875 per person (adjusted for inflation), a decline of 36%. Other Ohio cities that have lost population have been less successful at trimming their legacy debt burdens. Cleveland's long-term per capita debt burden more than doubled over this same period, as did Akron's, Toledo's, and nearby Springfield's. Dayton's success at decreasing its long-term debt bodes well for the city's future, since

22. Dayton's Comprehensive Annual Financial Reports, http://www.daytonohio.gov/DocumentCenter/.

23. Stephen Eide, "Rust Belt Cities and Their Burden of Legacy Costs" (Manhattan Institute Report, October 2017).

large long-term debts can force cities to cut services or neglect necessary infrastructure repairs as the cost of servicing that debt crowds out current spending.

Dayton's general fund revenues are largely dependent on local taxes. According to the city's audited Comprehensive Annual Financial Reports, the income tax generated nearly $700 per capita in 2016. In comparison, the property tax generated less than $100 per capita, as shown in figure 8.

From 2002 to 2016, income tax and property tax receipts together generated between 76% and 86% of all general fund revenue. The bulk of the revenue comes from the income tax, which generated approximately seven times the revenue per capita as the property tax during this period. Dayton's income tax rate is 2.25%, and the entire tax was made permanent after voters passed a referendum in 2015.[24]

As shown in figure 8, both income tax revenue per capita and property tax revenue per capita declined prior to 2010. Income tax revenue per capita started to decline in 2006 and continued to fall during the Great Recession, while property tax revenue did not start to decline until 2008, with a second dip in 2011. Both appear to have leveled off, but at levels that are substantially lower than in the early 2000s. The decline in revenue brought in by these taxes helps explain Dayton's overall decline in revenue per person from 2002 to 2016.

The housing bust that contributed to the Great Recession affected Dayton's property tax revenue. In 2014 real city property valuations were down 26% from their 2006 peak, and lower assessed property values decrease the property taxes owed, all else equal. The number of vacant housing properties in Dayton has also increased recently. In 2005 there were only 14,795 vacant housing properties in Dayton. At the peak of the recession in 2008 the number of vacant properties increased to just over 19,000, but by 2010 the amount had fallen to only 16,000. However, from 2010 to 2015 the amount of vacant properties rose again, up to 16,938 in 2015.

Vacancies hurt Dayton's finances in several ways. First, owners of vacant properties pay taxes at a lower rate than owner-occupiers. Second, vacant properties are often cared for by the city, which is a substantial expense in the summer months when lawns need to be maintained.[25] Finally, there's

24. "Dayton Voters Pass Issue 6 Making Income Tax Permanent," *Dayton Daily News*, May 6, 2014, http://www.mydaytondailynews.com/news/news/dayton-voters-to-decide-on-permanent-income-tax/nfqZn/.

25. Doug Page, "Local Governments Filing Liens against Lawns They Had to Mow," *Dayton Daily News*, September 1, 2013, http://www.mydaytondailynews.com/news/local-governments-filing-liens-against-lawns-they-had-mow/1xfJzGEW36CxPM12iPBObI/.

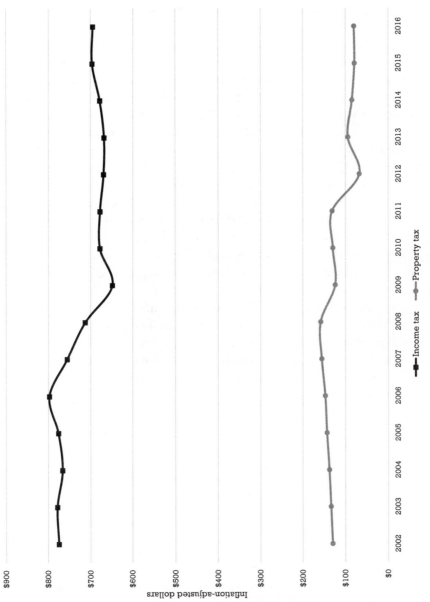

FIGURE 8. Dayton per capita tax revenue, 2002–2016, adjusted for inflation to 2009 dollars. (From Dayton's Comprehensive Annual Financial Reports.)

evidence that vacant properties owned by banks—known as real-estate-owned properties, or REOs—decrease the values of nearby homes when they fall into a state of disrepair. Lower home values lead to lower assessed values for property tax purposes, and this leads to less property tax revenue, which puts pressure on city budgets.[26]

As we have seen, Dayton's expenditures rose rapidly during the latter half of the twentieth century before leveling off in the 1990s. Some of this increase was likely due to the influence of public-sector unions, which tend to raise labor costs and hinder investment that increases worker productivity but eliminates positions. More recently, expenditures have declined along with the city's population and revenues. The main sources of tax revenue for the city, income taxes and property taxes, have recently generated less revenue than in the early 2000s, and it's important that the city continues to control expenditures so as not to find itself in a financial hole. Other northern cities, Chicago being a prime example, have been unable or unwilling to align their expenditures with their revenues, and as a result they are now facing tough financial decisions.[27] Dayton's relatively prudent behavior over the last 20 years has enabled it to maintain its infrastructure and city services while decreasing its long-term debt, thereby increasing the city's chances of economic success going forward.

Over the last two chapters we examined the causes of Dayton's population decline and reviewed the city's finances. In the next chapter, we will take a closer look at Dayton's current economy to see how the city is doing today. In terms of population, Dayton appears to have stabilized, but as we will see there are still signs of stress in the city's labor market.

26. Keith Ihlanfeldt and Tom Mayock, "Foreclosures and Local Government Budgets," *Regional Science and Urban Economics* 53 (2015): 135–47.

27. Monica Davey, "Chicago's Fiscal Problems Dog Rahm Emanuel's 2nd Term as Mayor," *New York Times*, September 8, 2015, https://www.nytimes.com/2015/09/09/us/chicago-fiscal-rahm-emanuel.html.

CHAPTER 6

Dayton's Economy Today and What It Can Do to Thrive Again

WE'VE EXAMINED the factors that contributed to Dayton's population and economic decline over the last 60 years, and we've examined the city's finances over the same period. But we haven't yet looked at the result of all the changes that took place in Dayton. That is, what does the city's economy and labor market look like today? The purpose of this chapter is to examine Dayton's economy today in order to establish a baseline from which to judge future economic changes. Next we will discuss some steps Dayton can take to once again become a thriving, innovative city.

Like other midwestern and northeastern US cities, the Dayton area's economy transitioned from a manufacturing economy to a service economy during the late twentieth century.

As shown in figure 9, the percentage of nonfarm, private sector employment in manufacturing in the Dayton metro area declined from 43% in 1969 to 20% in 2000. Meanwhile, the percentage of employment in services increased from 19% to 36%. These changes are similar to national changes over the same period. Across the country, manufacturing employment fell from 29% to 14% of all nonfarm, private sector employment while employment in services increased from 23% to 38%.

In the Dayton metro area, military and federal civilian employment also fell relative to all private nonfarm employment, which means the impor-

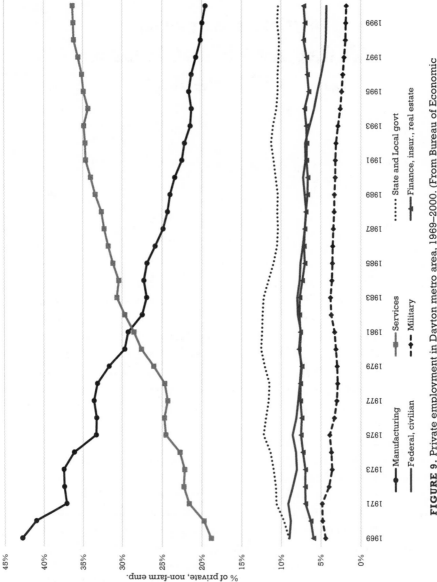

FIGURE 9. Private employment in Dayton metro area, 1969–2000. (From Bureau of Economic Analysis, US Department of Commerce, regional data, table CA25, Employment by industry.)

Legend:
- Manufacturing
- Federal, civilian
- Services
- Military
- State and Local govt
- Finance, insur., real estate

Y-axis: % of private, non-farm emp.

Values: 45%, 40%, 35%, 30%, 25%, 20%, 15%, 10%, 5%, 0%

X-axis: 1969, 1971, 1973, 1975, 1977, 1979, 1981, 1983, 1985, 1987, 1989, 1991, 1993, 1995, 1996, 1997, 1999

tance of federally funded workers to the Dayton metro area's labor force declined over this period. The percentage of metro area employment in finance, insurance, and real estate grew slightly over this period, while the percentage of employment in state and local government remained fairly constant at approximately 10%.

A look at the largest employers in the Dayton metro area (see figure 10) reinforces the broader data above. Despite the relative decline of federal civilian and military employment over time, Wright-Patterson Air Force Base remains the area's largest employer with over 27,000 employees—almost 8% of all employees in the metro area. The other large employers are primarily in health care, government, and education. This is very different from the 1950s, when manufacturing dominated and GM-affiliated factories alone accounted for a substantial portion of the metro area's nonfarm employment.

Additionally, there is a noticeable lack of technology, finance, insurance, and scientific/engineering firms. Firms in these industries typically benefit the most from the knowledge spillovers that occur in dense urban downtowns. Going forward, these industries, not manufacturing, will form the employment base of successful cities. Unfortunately for the city of Dayton, the only non-health, private-sector employer in the metro area's top 10 is LexisNexis, and it's located in Miamisburg, outside of Dayton's city limits. As we discussed earlier, agglomeration economies—the productivity benefits that accrue to workers and firms when they are in proximity to one another—raise wages and make firms more competitive, but they also dissipate with distance. For Dayton to fully reap the benefits of agglomeration economies and to thrive as an employment hub in the new knowledge economy, it will need some LexisNexis-type firms to locate within its city limits.

As we have discussed, the transition to a service and knowledge economy has not been easy on Dayton's economy, and the 2008–9 recession didn't help matters. During the Great Recession, Dayton lost a substantial amount of employment. The full-time civilian employed population in the city averaged around 31,900 each year from 2011 to 2016, which is considerably below the prerecession high of 38,000 or even the 2005–7 average of 35,000 employed people.[1] Median individual earnings for full-time civilian workers in Dayton have also yet to recover from their 2008 high of roughly $35,000 per year. They slightly rebounded to $34,189 in 2011 but declined again after that, and in 2016 they were $32,681. This decline in earnings has contributed to the city's lower income tax receipts that we noted previously.

---

1. American FactFinder, US Census Bureau, tables B24041 and S2404. Data from 2005 to 2008 are from one-year estimates; data from 2009 to 2015 are from five-year estimates.

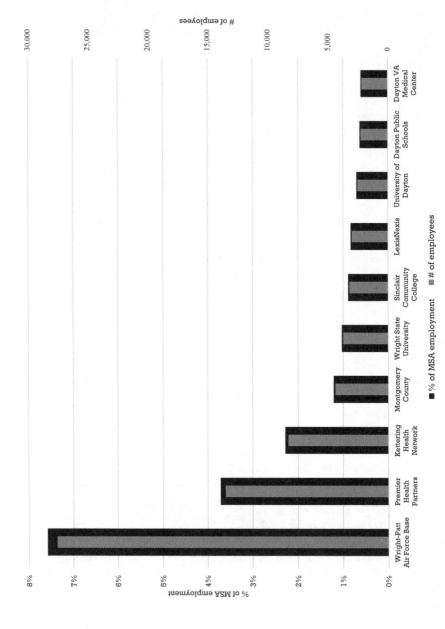

FIGURE 10. Ten largest employers in Dayton metro area in 2016. (From *Dayton Business Journal*, October 20, 2016.)

Over a longer horizon, the average wage in the Dayton metro area has been declining relative to the overall Ohio average wage as seen in figure 11. The figure depicts the metro area average annual wage divided by the Ohio average annual wage. A number greater than 1 indicates that the metro area average wage is greater than the statewide average wage. In 1969 the Dayton area had the highest average wage relative to the state of the six large Ohio metro areas: It was 10% higher.

Since then the Dayton metro area's ratio has declined, with a substantial drop occurring after the most recent recession in 2007. In 2016 its average wage was about the same as Akron's and below Cincinnati's, Cleveland's, and Columbus's. Cleveland's wage ratio has remained fairly constant, while Cincinnati's and Columbus's ratio increased dramatically, causing them to rise from fifth and sixth, respectively, into a tie for first. In 2016 the average wage in each of those metro areas was about 8% higher than the overall state average. Along with the population gains in the Columbus and Cincinnati metro areas we discussed previously, these wage data are evidence that Columbus and Cincinnati are the Ohio metro areas best adapting to the twenty-first-century economy.

Average wages in the metro areas of Toledo and Akron, two former manufacturing cities that have experienced many of the same problems as Dayton, have also declined relative to the state average over the last 40 plus years. Along with Dayton, these two metro areas are clustered separately from Cleveland, Columbus, and Cincinnati. The long-term decline in wages relative to the state average means it's unlikely that the Dayton metro area will experience any significant wage gains in the near future unless something changes.

Home values in the city of Dayton are falling relative to the surrounding metro area as well. In January 2008, near the start of the recession, the median single-family home value in Dayton was approximately 60% of the median home value in the surrounding metro area ($70,500 vs. $118,300).[2] Since then, the median home value in Dayton has declined relative to the surrounding area. In March 2017 it was only 49% ($55,700 vs. $114,200). The decline in home values negatively affects property tax revenue and helps explain the per capita property tax revenue decline.

Three common measures of a city's economic health are population, wages, and home values, and Dayton is performing poorly in all three. The lower rate of full-time employment since 2009, declining earnings, and

2. Home Values, Zillow Research, accessed February 7, 2019, http://www.zillow.com/research/data/.

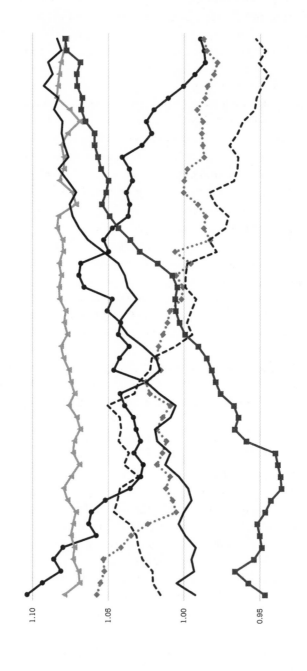

FIGURE 11. Average wage ratio by metro area, 1969–2016. (Data from the Bureau of Economic Analysis, US Department of Commerce, regional data, tables SA30 [Ohio] and CA30 [Metropolitan Statistical Areas].)

declining home values, coupled with a historically declining population, exemplify the economic and fiscal difficulties facing Dayton.

These measures of economic health are all related, which on the one hand is a good thing since if one measure improves it usually leads to improvement in the others. On the other hand, this interconnectedness makes improving one measure difficult since they reinforce one another. Population decline leads to empty homes and less government revenue, which leads to a decline in property values as city services worsen. Firm relocations decrease employment opportunities and often negatively impact wages. This leads to more population decline as people move to take higher paying jobs in more prosperous cities with better neighborhoods, further pushing down property values and starting the cycle over again.

Stopping this cycle has proven to be a difficult task. Researchers have proposed numerous solutions, and city officials in Dayton and around the country have tried many of them—sports stadiums, refurbished downtowns, tax incentives and abatements for businesses, and subsidized business parks—but as we discussed earlier such policies have been largely unsuccessful. Moreover, it has been difficult to duplicate the few success stories, which demonstrates the uniqueness of each city's problems despite apparent similarities. That said, there are some steps that Dayton officials can take to improve the city's chances of future success, and we will discuss them soon.

Joblessness and Opioids in Dayton

Before we discuss how Dayton can improve its economy, we need to address the city's latest problem. It's no secret that many cities in the Midwest are suffering from an opioid crisis largely driven by the increased use of synthetic opioids like Fentanyl. From 2013 to 2016, unintentional drug overdoses in Ohio due to Fentanyl increased from fewer than three per 100,000 people to 20 per 100,000 people.[3] According to data from 2015, white males between the ages of 25 and 44—prime working years—comprised most of the opioid-related overdose deaths in Ohio. Black males and white females between the same ages fatally overdosed at about half the rate of white males.

---

3. Dionissi Aliprantis and Anne Chen, "The Opioid Epidemic and the Labor Market," *Economic Commentary, Federal Reserve Bank of Cleveland,* September 29, 2017. https://www.clevelandfed.org/newsroom-and-events/publications/economic-commentary/2017-economic-commentaries/ec-201715-opioids.aspx.

The hardest-hit Ohio counties are in the northeast and southwest, and Dayton is at the center of it all. According to one study that used 2014 state health data and data from the Center for Disease Control and Prevention, Dayton had the highest rate of all overdose deaths in the country.[4] There were almost twice as many overdose deaths in Montgomery County by May 2017 as there were in all of 2016, which had been the record year. The county coroner's office located in Dayton's downtown had to expand in 2016, and the *New York Times* reported that the office had to temporarily store bodies in local funeral homes on several occasions.[5] Data for all of 2017 was not available at the time of this writing, but a preliminary report from the coroner's office indicated a continuing increase in overdose deaths.[6]

Nobel Prize–winning economist Angus Deaton and his colleague (and wife) Anne Case attribute some of the opioid problem to a wider problem that they call "deaths of despair."[7] In their research, they document a rising number of deaths due to opioids, alcohol, and suicide, primarily among working-age people without a college degree, and they think that economic conditions play a role. More recent preliminary research finds the link between the economy and the opioid epidemic weaker than implied by Deaton and Case, but economic conditions still matter.[8]

While the empirical research is ongoing, it is useful to think about how the economy and the opioid epidemic may be linked. In a 2017 essay in *City Journal,* Harvard economist Ed Glaeser noted that studies have found a large drop in happiness is associated with unemployment, and that unemployment leads to 45,000 suicides annually worldwide.[9] He also mentions that studies have found that the jobless spend less time socializing with others, more time watching television, and are more likely to use illegal drugs.

---

4. "These Are the Most Dangerous Drugged Out Cities in America," ArrestRecords .com, accessed February 7, 2019, http://www.arrestrecords.com/these-are-the-most -drugged-out-cities-in-america/.

5. Kimiko de Freytas-Tamura, "Amid Opioid Overdoses, Ohio Coroner's Office Runs Out of Room for Bodies," February 2, 2017, https://www.nytimes.com/2017/02/02/us/ ohio-overdose-deaths-coroners-office.html.

6. Research Update on Fentanyl Outbreaks in the Dayton, OH, Area, Wright State University, April 28, 2017, http://www.mcohio.org/Fentanyl_Outbreak_2017.pdf.

7. Angus Deaton, Economic Aspects of the Opioid Crisis: Testimony to the Joint Economic Committee of the US Congress, June 8, 2017, https://www.jec.senate.gov/public/ _cache/files/37cbd2d6-da98-4d92-87bb-cb2a7ed7b91d/deaton-testimony-060817.pdf.

8. Christopher J. Ruhm, *"Deaths of Despair or Drug Problems?"* (Working Paper No. 24188, National Bureau of Economic Research, 2018).

9. Edward L. Glaeser, "The War on Work—and How to End It," *City Journal,* 2017, https://www.city-journal.org/html/war-work-and-how-end-it-15250.html.

In their own research, Glaeser and fellow economist David Cutler find that the best predictor of the rise in opioid deaths from 1992 to 2012 is the share of the population on disability. To Glaeser, this suggests:

A combination of the direct influence of being disabled, which generates a demand for painkillers; the availability of the drugs through the health-care system; and the psychological misery of having no economic future.

This book has documented Dayton's economic decline over the last 60 years, and one of the results of this decline is that a large share of Dayton's working-age population is not working or even looking for work. In the Dayton metro area in 2016, 83% of people between the ages of 25 and 44 were categorized as being in the labor force, meaning they were either working or actively looking for work. But within Dayton's city limits, only 75% of 25- to 44-year-olds were in the labor force in 2016, down from 79% as recently as 2010.

Examining males only—since they have been hit hardest by the opioid crisis—just 68% of males between the ages of 20 and 64 were in the labor force in the city of Dayton in 2016, while 82% were in the labor force in the metro area overall. This tells us that the low labor force participation rate for working-age males is a bigger issue in Dayton than in other nearby cities such as Beavercreek, Kettering, Centerville, and Fairborn, which are all in the same metro area.

The biggest discrepancies in labor force participation rates between Dayton and the rest of the metro area are found at the lower education levels. About 85% of metro area residents between the ages of 25 and 64 with a bachelor's or advanced degree were in the labor force in both Dayton and the metro area in 2016. But for people within the same age range with a high school degree only, just 62% were in the labor force in Dayton while 72% were in the labor force in the metro area overall, a gap of 10 percentage points. This gap was only eight percentage points in 2010. There's also a big difference between the Dayton and the metro area labor force participation rates for people with less than a high school degree—47% in Dayton versus 53% in the metro area. And like the high school gap, Dayton has recently fallen further behind: In 2010 the labor force participation rate in Dayton for people without a high school degree was only three percentage points lower than the metro area's (53% versus 56%) rather than six (47% versus 53%).

Let's think about what these numbers mean. If only 68% of Dayton's males between the ages of 20 and 64 are in the labor force, meaning they are either working or looking for work, then 32%, or nearly one out of three,

aren't doing either of those things. So what are they doing? As we discussed
before, research finds that the jobless spend more time watching TV and less
time socializing with others. So about one-third of Dayton's working-age
males are probably spending a considerable amount of time alone in front
of their TV.

Work is associated with benefits other than income. For many of us,
work is part of what gives our lives a purpose. People often take pride in
their jobs and enjoy the feeling of being wanted by an employer. We also
form bonds with our coworkers, many of whom become friends or even a
significant other. Without a job, people need something else to fill the gap.
It's not hard to imagine that many unemployed people, particularly males
with little formal education, are filling this gap with drugs or alcohol. And
as these data show, joblessness and its associated problems are particularly
prevalent within Dayton's city limits.

How Dayton Can Thrive Again

In terms of wages and employment, Dayton's economy has been deteriorating for decades. More recently, the city of Dayton was hit hard by the
Great Recession and now faces an opioid problem and a high rate of joblessness among the city's working-age males. So what can Dayton do to once
again become a thriving city? Earlier we discussed the importance of high
human capital to a city's success, and in the modern service and knowledge
economy entrepreneurship and innovation are critical components of any
city's economic well-being. If Dayton is going to be reinvented, it will need a
skilled labor force that can continuously create new businesses and develop
new products as old ones are made obsolete by global competition and technological change.

Unfortunately, we saw that Dayton fell behind many other cities in its
share of educated residents in the mid-twentieth century, and relative to
other Ohio cities its situation has not improved. As shown in figure 12, the
Dayton metro area had the second lowest proportion of adults with a bachelor's degree or more in Ohio in 2016, ahead of only Toledo.[10] And just a
reminder, it's the human capital of a city's workforce that really matters for
growth, but educational attainment is a useful proxy.

The Columbus metro area, which contains the largest and fastest growing big city in the state, is well ahead of the Cleveland, Akron, and Cincin-

---

10. American FactFinder, US Census Bureau, table S1501, five-year estimates.

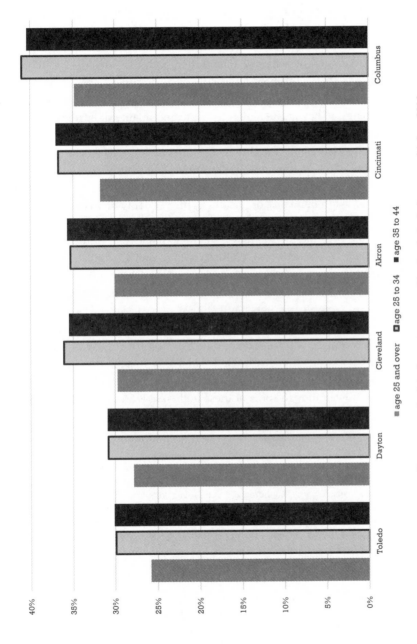

■ age 25 and over ■ age 25 to 34 ■ age 35 to 44

FIGURE 12. Percentage of adults in metro areas with a bachelor's degree or higher, 2016

nati metro areas clustered together in second place. The discrepancy between Dayton, Cincinnati, and Columbus is even larger at the city level. Only 18% of adults in the city of Dayton had a bachelor's degree or more in 2016, compared to 34% in the city of Cincinnati and 35% in the city of Columbus.

Economists Yong Chen and Stuart Rosenthal argue that educated high-skill workers follow a life-cycle migration path that involves locating in a city with a strong business environment during their working years and then moving to a location with attractive consumer amenities as retirement approaches.[11] They create a quality of life and quality of business index for 346 US metropolitan and nonmetropolitan areas. In their analysis, climate appears to be the most important consumer amenity, as nine of the areas in the top 10 of the quality of life index are in California or Hawaii, while only four of the top 20 are in cold-weather states.[12] Using data from 2000, Dayton is ranked 278th in quality of life and 135th in quality of business.

According to this ranking, Dayton had the second-worst business environment out of the metro areas in its region, ahead of only Toledo, which ranked 173. Cleveland (91), Columbus (94), and Cincinnati (96) had the highest business environment rankings of the Ohio metro areas. Nearby Indianapolis, Indiana, was ranked 103. The quality of life indicators for each metro area were all relatively low, between 244 (Akron) and 311 (Cincinnati), which is to be expected when looking at metro areas in colder areas. Since an area's climate is largely determined by factors outside of human control, local officials in poor climate locations such as Dayton must focus on improving their business environments in order to attract high-skill workers.[13] And even though some of these high-skill workers will leave one day

11. Yong Chen and Stuart S. Rosenthal, "Local Amenities and Life-Cycle Migration: Do People Move for Jobs or Fun?," *Journal of Urban Economics* 64, no. 3 (November 2008): 519–37.

12. Other authors have also found that nice weather and proximity to the coast are attractive features. For example, see David Albouy and Bert Lue, "*Driving to Opportunity: Local Rents, Wages, Commuting and Sub-Metropolitan Quality of Life,*" *Journal of Urban Economics* 89 (September 2015): 74–92; Liang Zheng, "What City Amenities Matter in Attracting Smart People?," *Papers in Regional Science* 95 (June 2016): 309–27.

13. Dayton's cold weather may reduce the city's attractiveness today, but it was not always viewed as a negative characteristic. In a letter written to the Men's Boosters' Club of Dayton in 1907, John H. Patterson wrote the following in reference to the difficulty of attracting talented workers to Dayton:

> Besides this, people we want to come with us claim that the climate of Dayton is bad on account of the heat and sultry weather of July, August, September, and part of October.
> It would be worth a good deal to our Company to be located in some city where it is not so hot in summer, as it naturally affects the work of our people, for they cannot do as much work or effectual work, as they

to retire in sunny Florida or Arizona, during their working years they will make Dayton a more productive and innovative place.

There's also a measure of economic freedom at the metro level that corroborates the Dayton metro area's middling ranking in the business climate index. This economic freedom index is designed to provide a measure of the obstacles (or encouragements) to productivity faced by workers and businesses.[14] The index includes measures of an area's tax burden, size of government, and labor market freedom. Of the 384 metro areas that are ranked, Dayton ranks 334, behind Columbus (321) and Akron (330) but ahead of Toledo (335) and Cleveland (347). Additional studies have found that metro areas with better scores on this metro area economic freedom index experience more per capita income growth and population growth than similar metro areas with worse scores.[15] This is more evidence that Dayton's best hope for future economic success is to create an economic environment that allows high human-capital workers and entrepreneurs to create and produce new products and services.

Research has shown that even in regions with declining populations new businesses are an important generator of employment growth.[16] But new businesses require entrepreneurs who are willing to take risks. Burdensome tax and regulatory policies stifle entrepreneurship and constrain Dayton's ability to compete in the global economy. In two recent studies of state business climate indices, the authors find that indices that emphasize taxes and the costs of doing business are able to predict economic growth, though not as much as industry composition or climate.[17] But as they note, the latter

could in a cooler climate. ("What Dayton, Ohio, Should do to Become a Model City," John H. Patterson speech, March 19, 1896, http://www.daytonhistorybooks.com/page/page/4390483.htm)

14. Dean B. Stansel, "An Economic Freedom Index for US Metropolitan Areas," *Journal of Regional Analysis and Policy* 43, no. 1 (2013): 3–20.

15. Jamie Bologna, Andrew T. Young, and Donald J. Lacombe, "A Spatial Analysis of Incomes and Institutional Quality: Evidence from US Metropolitan Areas," *Journal of Institutional Economics* 12, no. 1 (March 2016): 191–216; Adam A. Millsap, "The Role of Economic Freedom in Intercity Competition: A Framework and Some Evidence from US Metropolitan Areas," *Journal of Regional Analysis and Policy* 48, no. 2 (2018): 89–106.

16. Heike Delfmann and Sierdjan Koster, "The Effect of New Business Creation on Employment Growth in Regions Facing Population Decline," *Annals of Regional Science* 56, no. 1 (2016): 33–54.

17. Jed Kolko, David Neumark, and Marisol Cuellar Mejia, "What Do Business Climate Indexes Teach Us about State Policy and Economic Growth?," *Journal of Regional Science* 53, no. 2 (2013): 220–55; Georgeanne M. Artz et al., "Do State Business Climate Indicators Explain Relative Economic Growth at State Borders?," *Journal of Regional Science* 56, no. 3 (2016): 395–419.

factors are less amenable to policy (especially climate) meaning that policy makers who reside in less attractive areas should focus on improving their business environments if they want to foster economic growth.

The business environment and economic freedom measures discussed here apply to the entire metro area, not just the city of Dayton, so Dayton will need help to significantly improve the metro area's competitiveness. But as the biggest city in the area, Dayton can set an example. Furthermore, the surrounding cities will likely have to adjust their own policies in response to any improvements Dayton makes in order to remain competitive places to work and do business, which should improve the entire area's business climate over time.

Tax Policy

There is substantial evidence from regional and national studies that high-income workers, who tend to be skilled and mobile, are attracted to areas with low income taxes so long as government service quality, especially schools, do not suffer.[18] High marginal tax rates reduce the incentive to create value, and a complex tax code increases the cost of doing business through greater compliance costs that include both time and money expenses. Complex tax codes also require individuals to spend more of their time complying and less time doing other things they enjoy. The sensitivity of high-skill people to income taxes and service quality means that local governments that want to improve their economies need to focus on providing quality government services at the lowest possible cost.

At the state level, Ohio has eight income tax brackets and a top marginal rate of 4.99% that applies to incomes over $213,350.[19] Dayton's income tax rate is 2.25%, meaning that someone who earns more than $213,350 per year and works in Dayton would face a top marginal rate of 7.24% when combined with Ohio's top rate. Meanwhile, the four largest nearby cities of Kettering, Fairborn, Beavercreek, and Huber Heights have income tax rates of 2.25%, 1.5%, 0%, and 2.25%, respectively.[20] Only Kettering and Huber

---

18. Marius Brülhart, Sam Bucovetsky, and Kurt Schmidheiny, "Taxes in Cities," *Handbook of Regional and Urban Economics* 5 (2015): 1123–96.

19. "Ohio Individual Income Tax Rates: 2005–2018," Ohio Department of Taxation, accessed February 8, 2019, https://www.tax.ohio.gov/ohio_individual/individual/annual_tax_rates.aspx.

20. "Downloadable Municipal Income Tax Rate Database Table," Ohio Department of Taxation, accessed February 8, 2019, https://thefinder.tax.ohio.gov/StreamlineSalesTaxWeb/Download/MuniRateTableInstructions.aspx.

Heights have rates as high as Dayton's, which hurts Dayton's relative attractiveness as a place for doing business.

In addition to its relatively high income tax rate, Dayton also has a relatively high sales tax burden, though this rate is set at the county level. The state of Ohio has a 5.75% sales tax rate,[21] but Montgomery County also levies a 1% sales tax and a 0.5% transit tax, making the total sales tax burden in Dayton 7.25%. In adjacent Greene County, the rate is 6.75% and in Hamilton County, where Cincinnati is located, the rate is 7%.[22] Higher sales taxes reduce consumers' purchasing power and at the margin induce consumers to purchase goods and services in nearby lower-tax areas.

Property taxes are difficult to compare across cities due to the overlapping jurisdictions of school districts, cities, counties, and other special purpose governments. Still, in 2012 the *Dayton Daily News* compiled property tax data from 99 communities in four counties in Ohio and calculated the property tax burden as a percentage of median home value for these municipalities.[23] Dayton's property tax burden as a percentage of median home value was 2.16%, slightly lower than in Huber Heights (2.31%), Kettering (2.24%), and Beavercreek (2.17%).

Smartasset.com calculated the average effective property tax rate for all Ohio counties and Montgomery County's was 2.05% while adjacent Greene County's was 1.68%.[24] Smartasset also created an index meant to capture how efficiently a county spends its property tax revenue. Out of the 88 Ohio counties, Montgomery County ranked 82nd while adjacent Greene County ranked 66th. This is evidence that there's some room to increase efficiency in Montgomery County's municipalities, which means cities like Dayton can lower taxes while maintaining the quality of their government services.

Overall, the taxes faced by Dayton's residents are relatively high compared to the surrounding communities, through part of this discrepancy is at the county level and thus outside of Dayton's immediate control. Dayton officials should continuously look for ways to reduce their income tax and property tax rates in a way that does not undermine the city's ability to pro-

21. "Taxes in Ohio," Tax Foundation, https://taxfoundation.org/state/ohio/.

22. "Total State and Local Sales Tax Rates by County, 2018," October 1, 2018, Ohio Department of Taxation, http://www.tax.ohio.gov/portals/o/tax_analysis/tax_data_series/sales_and_use/salestaxmapcolor.pdf.

23. Joanne Huist Smith, "Snapshot of Property Taxes by County," *Dayton Daily News*, updated October 28, 2012, http://www.daytondailynews.com/news/news/state-regional-govt-politics/how-does-your-community-stack-up-a-snapshot-of-pro/nSn3J/.

24. "Ohio Property Tax Calculator," SmartAsset, accessed February 9, 2019, https://smartasset.com/taxes/ohio-property-tax-calculator.

vide basic services. This means they should objectively review what they do and how they do it in order to increase efficiency, thereby allowing them to reduce taxes and increase the city's economic competitiveness. One option is to end the use of firm-specific tax subsidies and abatements, such as those given to the Dayton Dragons and Fuyao Glass. Instead of individual tax subsidies for specific firms, Dayton officials could lower rates for everybody. This would create a fairer business climate and keep the government out of the business of picking winners and losers.

Differences in tax rates and tax policies across cities affect economic growth, but the already low rates in most cities don't give officials a lot of room to work with. Still, there are always opportunities for governments at all levels to make their tax policy more efficient, even if the resulting benefits—higher wages and more economic growth—are likely to be relatively small at the local level. And of course, higher tax rates or new taxes in Dayton that don't generate a corresponding improvement in city services should be avoided since they don't help the city's business climate.

Business Climate and Regulation

Because tax rates in Dayton are fairly low compared to state and federal tax rates, reducing regulation is likely to have a larger effect on economic activity within the city than tax cuts. Moreover, unlike tax cuts, decreasing regulation typically doesn't reduce a city's revenue, and revenue losses without compensating spending cuts or efficiency improvements will harm a city in the long run. In fact, reducing regulation should generate more revenue for Dayton, since theory and evidence suggest that reducing regulation increases innovation and new economic activity, which means more tax dollars.[25]

Many regulations impose fixed costs on entrepreneurs, meaning entrepreneurs must spend a certain amount of time and money to comply with the regulation regardless of how much output they are producing. A liquor permit is a good example. In Ohio, liquor permits are issued by the state and range in price from under $400 for the right to sell only beer to $20,000 for a casino that wants to serve alcohol.[26] These amounts may not sound ter-

25. James B. Bailey and Diana W. Thomas, "Regulating Away Competition: The Effect of Regulation on Entrepreneurship and Employment," *Journal of Regulatory Economics* 52, no. 3 (December 2017): 237–54.

26. Liquor Permit Classes, Ohio Department of Commerce, accessed February 9, 2019, http://www.com.ohio.gov/liqr/permitClasses.aspx.

ribly expensive, but in practice liquor permits often cost much more since the quantity is capped by the state based on population density. If an area has already reached its limit, a business that wants a liquor permit must purchase one from a business that's willing to sell.[27] This typically means purchasing the entire business, not just the permit, at a cost of hundreds of thousands or even millions of dollars.

Because the price of the license is determined by the type of establishment and the type of alcohol being sold rather than the quantity sold, business that sell more can spread the cost of a license over more sales. The more drinks sold, the smaller the cost added to each drink due to the cost of the license.

Since the average cost falls as more drinks are sold, the cost of a license is a bigger burden to small retailers than larger ones. Other regulations and licenses work in a similar way. So as the regulatory burden increases, we would expect it to have a bigger effect on the viability of small businesses than larger ones and that appears to be the case. The increase in fixed costs caused by more regulation also contributes to sluggish job growth since there is evidence that small businesses—which are typically affected most by the costs of regulation—create more jobs on average than larger businesses.[28] If regulation continues to favor larger business over smaller ones, we should expect weaker job growth going forward. Cities like Dayton can push back against this trend and create an economic advantage by streamlining their regulation.

Reducing regulation can also send a message to potential entrepreneurs about how Dayton views risk. There is evidence that urban areas that have an accepting attitude about risk are more innovative.[29] The implication is that cities can gain a competitive edge by attracting risk-loving individuals who increase the probability of innovation occurring in the city. One way for a city to attract high-skill entrepreneurs and foster innovation is to implement a policy of permissionless innovation. Tech researcher Adam Thierer writes that permissionless innovation "is the notion that experimentation with new technologies and business models should generally be permit-

27. "How to Transfer a Liquor Permit," Ohio Department of Commerce, Division of Liquor Control, accessed February 9, 2019, https://www.com.ohio.gov/documents/LIQR_HowToTransfer.pdf.

28. David Neumark, Brandon Wall, and Junfu Zhang, "Do Small Businesses Create More Jobs? New Evidence for the United States from the National Establishment Time Series," *Review of Economics and Statistics* 93, no. 1 (February 2011): 16–29.

29. Andrea Caragliu et al., "The Winner Takes It All: Forward-Looking Cities and Urban Innovation," *Annals of Regional Science* 56, no. 3 (May 2016): 617–45.

ted by default."[30] This is an alternative to current city regulatory regimes that rely on the precautionary principle, which is based on the idea that because some new products, services, or technologies may cause harm, their creators need to demonstrate their safety before bringing them to market. Local regulations that follow the precautionary principle include occupational licensing, business licensing, liquor licensing, and many zoning laws. For example, Dayton's zoning ordinance is over 400 pages long and includes prohibitions in a variety of areas, such as minimum lot sizes, the allowable uses of property, the height and material composition of fencing, and the minimum and maximum heights for buildings.[31]

Technological innovation is increasing at a faster pace than ever, but local regulations force entrepreneurs to fit their new products and services into a regulatory system designed for a slower-paced industrial economy rather than our modern faster-paced service and knowledge economy. Regulatory regimes based on the precautionary principle stifle innovation and entrepreneurship by limiting the trial-and-error process. New products and services will always have kinks that need to be worked out, but as Thierer says "trying to preemptively plan for every hypothetical worst case scenario means that many of the best-case scenarios will never come about." A citywide policy of permissionless innovation is a conspicuous sign of a city's positive attitude toward risk-taking and can help attract the risk-loving entrepreneurs cities need to be successful. Such a policy would position Dayton as a place of innovation and help drive long-term prosperity.

Earlier I pointed out that Dayton's climate is a disadvantage and that the city will have to compensate for a relatively poor climate by creating a much better business environment. Because Ohio has a robust home-rule law, city officials in Dayton have more control over the local business environment than city officials in many other states.[32] This gives them an opportunity to create a laboratory of innovation. The physical and social infrastructure is already in place—roads, buildings, an airport, universities, parks, police protection, and property rights. What is missing are the innovative, high-skill entrepreneurs capable of creating new goods and services that satisfy the unmet desires of consumers. In fact, many potential entrepreneurs may

30. Adam Thierer, "Permissionless Innovation: The Continuing Case for Comprehensive Technological Freedom," Mercatus Center at George Mason University, 2016.

31. City of Dayton, Ohio, Zoning Code, amended July 5, 2017, https://www.daytonohio.gov/DocumentCenter/View/550/City-of-Dayton-Zoning-Code-PDF?bidId.

32. Jesse J. Richardson, Meghan Zimmerman Gough, and Robert Puentes, "*Is Home Rule the Answer?: Clarifying the Influence of Dillon's Rule on Growth Management*," Center on Urban and Metropolitan Policy, the Brookings Institution, January 1 2003. Ohio is ranked 11 out of 49 in discretionary authority assigned to cities.

already be in the city but are too discouraged by red tape and regulatory hurdles to take the risky step of starting or expanding a business.

Additionally, research shows that local entrepreneurs cluster together in neighborhoods within cities and that entrepreneurial behavior reinforces itself via social interactions.[33] People who see successful entrepreneurs enjoying what they do may be inspired to start a small business themselves. Witnessing entrepreneurial success also makes the task seem less daunting, and successful entrepreneurs provide a potential source of guidance and advice for those just starting out. Over time, neighborhoods with a relatively high concentration of entrepreneurs can foster additional entrepreneurs, and this effect may spillover into nearby neighborhoods. The crucial task for policy makers is to create an environment that enables this process to occur.

Measuring the amount of regulation and its effect on economic activity at any level of government is difficult, but it is an especially challenging task at the state and local level due to the number of jurisdictions and paucity of available data. However, there have been efforts to do so and the measures are continuously improving. One recent study by the Pacific Research Institute ranked the 50 states based on their small-business regulatory burden.[34] The ranking consisted of 14 components that impact small businesses, including workers' compensation insurance, occupational licensing requirements, minimum wage laws, right-to-work laws, and land-use regulations among others. And though this is a state ranking, it still has implications for Dayton.

Ohio was ranked 27, just in front of Michigan and behind Kentucky. Indiana, Ohio's neighbor to the west, was ranked 1. To the extent that this ranking is accurate, it means Ohio cities, especially those close to the Indiana border like Dayton, are at a disadvantage. Local officials should pressure state officials to remove the barriers and restrictions that prevent them from effectively competing with nearby out-of-state cities.

At the local level, the consumer service website Thumbtack has conducted a small-business friendliness survey since 2012.[35] The 2015 results were based on the responses of nearly 18,000 small-business owners from around the country. This survey grades states and metro areas in 10 differ-

33. Martin Andersson and Johan P. Larsson, "Local Entrepreneurship Clusters in Cities," *Journal of Economic Geography* 16, no. 1 (January 2016): 39–66.

34. Wayne Winegarden, "The 50-State Small Business Regulation Index," *Pacific Research Institute*, July 2015.

35. Thumbtack: 2015 Small Business Survey, accessed February 9, 2019, https://www.thumbtack.com/survey#/2015/1/states. The survey was conducted in 2016 and 2017 as well, but those years did not include grades for the Dayton metro area.

ent categories, including ease of starting a business, ease of hiring, regulations, zoning, and the tax code, among others. The Dayton area received an
overall grade of A- in 2014 and B- in 2015. It ranked poorly on ease of hiring
and environmental regulations in both years and fared poorly on health and
safety regulations in 2015. As for the other large Ohio metro areas, Columbus received an A- in 2015, Cleveland a C+, Cincinnati a B- , and Akron a B.

Survey data are not a perfect measure of a city's regulatory burden, but
they do tell us something about how small-business owners view the burden
in their city. This is important since perception can affect reality. As noted
previously, aspiring entrepreneurs often look to established entrepreneurs
for guidance, and if Dayton's current small-business owners think operating
a business is hard they may discourage others who ask them for advice. The
survey results from Thumbtack reveal that there is room for improvement
in Dayton.

We can also think about Dayton's current regulatory environment this
way: In the early 1900s the Wright brothers flew a plane over Huffman
Prairie without asking any government official if it was OK. They also conducted all their research and test flights without any government subsidies
or permits. The result of their nongovernment-sanctioned, nongovernment-
funded risk-taking was a series of scientific breakthroughs that changed the
world. Could something like this happen in Dayton, or any other city for
that matter, today?

There are three broad policies Dayton officials can implement to regain a
climate of permissionless innovation like the one the Wright brothers, John
Patterson, Edward Deeds, and Charles Kettering thrived in. These are the
innovator's presumption, the sunsetting imperative, and the parity provision.[36] Together, these policies will help foster innovation and entrepreneurship in Dayton.

The *innovator's presumption* is the idea that any person or regulatory body
who opposes a new technology, product, or service must demonstrate why
it's in the public's interest to regulate it instead of requiring the innovator
to demonstrate why the innovation is safe. By placing the burden of proof
on the person who objects to the innovation, Dayton can temper impulsive
regulation based on hypothetical, worst-case scenarios.

Sunsetting is a term used to describe laws or regulations that expire after
a set period of time, say two years after enactment. In order for the regulation to stay on the books, officials must take a vote or some other action. Sun-

---

36. Thierer, "Permissionless Innovation."

setting rules force officials to periodically reevaluate rules and regulations to ensure that they are still relevant and are working as intended. Dayton should implement a sunsetting provision for two reasons: (1) to prevent regulations from needlessly accumulating and (2) to give officials regularly scheduled opportunities to replace or reform regulations that aren't performing.

Finally, the *parity provision* calls for all businesses in an industry to be regulated no more than the least regulated business. For example, ridesharing companies Uber and Lyft drastically disrupted the taxi and limo industries by offering customers a cheaper and easier alternative for securing a ride from point A to point B. In response, many taxi and limo companies complained that Uber and Lyft weren't playing by the same rules and called for them to be regulated just like taxi and limo companies. But this has it backwards. The parity provision says that instead of regulating Uber and Lyft up to the level of taxi and limo companies, taxi and limo companies should be regulated down to the level of Uber and Lyft. This would put all businesses in this industry on the same playing field and allow them to compete with one another by offering better quality at lower prices. This is a better scenario for both consumers and workers than having businesses try to push the government to regulate their competitors out of existence.

Like medical doctors, city officials in charge of regulation should strive to "First, do no harm." It is important for regulators to exercise patience before regulating to give themselves time to fully understand the pros and cons of new technology. Humility is also important, since even the most well-informed regulator lacks complete knowledge and the ability to see the future. Some immediate regulatory action may be necessary, but incremental regulation that addresses specific, tangible, immediate problems is less likely to stifle the development of new and better products and services than sweeping bans enacted due to fears of hypothetical, worst-case scenarios. And when regulation is enacted, it should be periodically reevaluated to ensure that it is performing as expected and still needed. Regulations that are left on the books but functionally obsolete due to the rapid pace of technological progress increase costs and uncertainty for entrepreneurs who still must spend time and money complying. A sunset provision that mandates reevaluation helps clean up municipal regulatory codes, which allows business owners to focus on complying with the regulations that actually matter for public safety.

As I have argued in my own research, because firms and industries in any city are eventually challenged by new competitors, we need to understand how cities deal with such challenges in order to understand how they thrive over time.[37] Differences in policies across cities generate differences in growth and development since different policies have different effects on the ability of local firms to adapt to change. Cities that implement or maintain policies that make it easier for entrepreneurs to generate new activities to replace the old should have more resilient economies and better economic outcomes than similar cities that hinder adaptation and innovation.

Other researchers have also commented on the effects that regulations, rules, and policies have on city growth. Harvard Business School professor Michael Porter argues that altering rules and regulations to create a favorable environment for business can help generate economic development in cities.[38] Economic geographer Michael Storper also suggests that local-level rules and regulations could be the key forces that enable or stifle economic specialization and development in cities.[39] Dayton officials can implement the policies of permissionless innovation—the innovator's presumption, the sunsetting imperative, and the parity provision—to update the city's regulatory environment in a way that encourages economic growth.

In the long run, Dayton, or any other city, should not hinge its hopes on large, footloose companies to serve as employment anchors. If a company can be attracted by a tax-incentive package, it's also likely to leave when the incentives end. Dayton needs local entrepreneurs to plant a thousand seeds and wait for some to take root.

As we noted earlier, Dayton has a university and a large community college in its city limits and another university nearby. Dayton officials need to implement policies that improve the city's chances of retaining the graduates of these schools in order to increase the average skill level of its workforce. If Dayton is going to successfully compete with larger cities that provide more amenities, better weather, or a higher-skilled workforce, it must do a better job of retaining the top talent from the area. Dayton needs a new John Patterson and Charles Kettering.

Homegrown entrepreneurs and high-skill workers who have social and familial ties to the area are also more likely to remain in Dayton than those attracted by temporary tax breaks. And if they do migrate at a relatively young age to seek fame and fortune elsewhere, they are more inclined to return upon attaining success. For example, economist Enrico Moretti

---

37. Adam A. Millsap, "The Role of Economic Freedom in Intercity Competition," 89–106.

38. Michael E. Porter, "New Strategies for Inner-City Economic Development," *Economic Development Quarterly* 11, no. 1 (1998): 11–27.

39. Michael Storper, "Why Do Regions Develop and Change? The Challenge for Geography and Economics," *Journal of Economic Geography* (2011): 333–46.

reports in his book, *The New Geography of Jobs,* that Bill Gates and Paul Allen decided to return to Seattle from Albuquerque, New Mexico, after launching Microsoft because they were originally from the area.[40]

Historic Districts

One of the first areas Dayton officials should reexamine as part of a policy of permissionless innovation is the city's land-use regulations, starting with the city's historic districts. Like other cities its age, Dayton has several codified historic districts: As of 2016 there were 20 historic districts containing over 2,900 buildings in a city of only about 140,000 people.[41] Dayton's Landmark Commission is charged with reviewing and approving major modifications to the buildings in historic districts, including their demolition. Many of the districts are located near the center of the city and contain homes built in the late 1800s and early 1900s. Some of the districts are also quite large: St. Anne's Hill contains 315 structures and the South Park Historic District covers 24 blocks and contains more than 700 structures. Seventy percent of the districts are protected by a local historic designation, which is the strictest, while 30% are protected only by the national designation.

The age of Dayton's downtown housing stock—which includes many old homes protected by historic district status—is likely holding the city back. The theory behind this idea is simple: High-income people want nice housing, and nice housing tends to be new housing. Because cities grow out from a central location, housing near the center tends to be older than housing further out. As a result, we should generally expect higher-income people to move out of downtown locations with old housing and into more suburban locations with new housing. A study that examined this theory found evidence supporting it.[42]

This is not necessarily bad news for downtown locations. In the latter half of the twentieth century, buying new housing meant buying suburban homes. But as suburban housing ages and new housing is built to replace the even older housing in the central city, high-income people should be drawn back to downtown neighborhoods. This has the power to reduce the

40. Enrico Moretti, *The New Geography of Jobs,* 75.

41. "Historic Preservation," City of Dayton, accessed February 9, 2019, http://www.daytonohio.gov/717/Historic-Preservation.

42. Jan K. Brueckner and Stuart S. Rosenthal, "Gentrification and Neighborhood Housing Cycles: Will America's Future Downtowns Be Rich?," *Review of Economics and Statistics* 91, no. 4 (November 2009): 725–43.

income disparity between the central city and suburbs that exists in many metropolitan areas.

This sounds reasonable, but there is one problem: Historic districts prevent old downtown housing from being torn down. In a free market for housing, old housing would be torn down and replaced by new housing once the net benefits of demolition and rebuilding exceed the net benefits of renovation. And a lot of downtown real estate in older cities should be replaced. A 2013 study that examined the Cleveland housing market determined that it's economical to demolish more than half of the older vacant homes rather than renovate them.[43]

But in historic districts, the housing is protected by local rules that limit demolitions and the types of renovations that can be undertaken since property owners are required to maintain their home's historic exterior. These rules create several barriers to downtown revitalization. First, older homes, especially those built prior to 1940, are expensive to restore and maintain. They often have outdated plumbing systems, electrical systems, and inefficient windows that need to be replaced. They may also contain lead paint or other hazardous materials commonly used at the time they were built but may have to be removed. Many people can't afford these upfront costs and those who can often don't want to deal with the hassle of a restoration project.

Second, people have different tastes. Unfortunately, historic districts freeze the housing stock based on the tastes people had 100 years ago. Old homes can be charming, but some people like ultra-modern homes, while others might just want to rent an apartment in a new building with modern amenities. For the people who want something other than a 100-year-old home, historic districts aren't an option.

Dayton's historic districts are also problematic because of their location. Many of Dayton's historic districts are located near the center of the city in the most walkable neighborhoods. The Oregon District, St. Anne's Hill, Huffman, and South Park are all located in areas that could be thriving hot spots of downtown living. The Oregon District already has a reputation as a trendy neighborhood, but whenever I go there I can't help but wonder what it could be if all its buildings weren't considered sacred—if there were more mixed-use development, more density due to more apartments and fewer homes, and more modern store fronts. The same can be said about all these neighborhoods.

---

43. Frank Ford et al., "The Role of Investors in the One-to-Three Family REO Market: The Case of Cleveland," *Washington, DC, What Works Collaborative*, 2013.

Recent research finds that downtowns in the largest metro areas are in the midst of a revival. Between 2000 and 2010, college-educated people between the ages of 25 and 34 flocked to the downtowns of the 50 largest metro areas.[44] The population of people aged 35 to 44 also increased in these downtowns but at a slower rate than for the younger group. In my own research, I find that millennials with a college degree are more likely to locate in high-amenity, walkable central cities such as New York, Chicago, and Portland than baby boomers when there were of a similar age.[45]

As we discussed earlier, the thick labor markets in cities make them attractive to specialized workers, which is one reason why there are so many college graduates in cities. But there are also consumption benefits that come with living in a large city. More people means more potential customers, and this means that specialized shops, bars, and restaurants are more likely to succeed in large, dense cities than in less populated areas. Moreover, it turns out that the presence of consumption options that require a person to be present to enjoy them—and which economists call "non-tradeable goods" because it's difficult to move them across space—is what is driving the recent urban revival. Amenities like specialized restaurants, bars, and gyms are appealing to young college-educated adults who are staying single and childless longer than previous generations, and such amenities explain most of the recent resurgence of downtowns.

The Dayton metro area's size places it out of the top 50 (its rank can change yearly but it's around 70), but that doesn't mean it can't benefit from these trends. The downtown area is already livelier than it used to be, with breweries such as Toxic Brew Company, Warped Wing, 5th Street Brewpub, and the Dayton Beer Company—all of which opened in the last decade or so—drawing people downtown on Saturday and Sunday afternoons. A visitor from Boston, Manhattan, or Washington, DC, might not be impressed with the size of the crowds, but there's a noticeable difference compared to just a few years ago and that's a good sign. If Dayton wants to build on this momentum, it needs to be more flexible when it comes to building.

If a couple wants to buy a historic house and renovate it they should be free to do so, but they should also be allowed to build a new structure on the property. When a city protects large swaths of buildings in historic districts, it slows down the cycle of housing construction that can draw people to walkable urban neighborhoods. This is especially true if the historic dis-

44. Victor Couture and Jessie Handbury, "*Urban Revival in America, 2000 to 2010*" (Working Paper No. 24084, National Bureau of Economic Research, 2017).

45. Adam Millsap, "Location Choice in Early Adulthood: Millennials versus Baby Boomers," *Papers in Regional Science* 97 (2018): S139–S167.

tricts encompass the most enticing areas of the city, such as those closest to downtown amenities and employment opportunities. Living in the city is appealing to many people, but being forced to purchase and live in outdated housing dampens the appeal.

Critics might correctly point out that cities like Boston, New York, and Washington, DC, have lots of old homes and they're doing well, but that's the wrong way to interpret the housing stocks of those cities. A better interpretation is that they are doing well despite their old housing stocks, not because of them. People live in cities for a variety of reasons, and cities that have a lot of good things going for them can afford some growth-retarding policies. For example, all those cities have several of the top universities in the world either in their city limits or just outside them, and the universities draw in tens of thousands of high-skilled, high human-capital people to those cities every year. If Dayton had similar institutions drawing thousands of young people downtown every year, it's housing stock wouldn't matter as much since the demand for space would be high for reasons that have little to do with the housing itself. But it doesn't. Instead, Dayton must maximize its potential, and allowing newer housing in the most desirable neighborhoods is a step in that direction.

The major theme of this book is that successful cities are places of innovation and specialization that must be able to adapt to changing economic circumstances. Such adaptation is difficult, which is why many cities fail at it, but it's even more difficult when the city's built environment is frozen in time. If Dayton wants to be a city of the future, it needs to let go of some of its past.

Immigrants and Cities

Dayton needs new housing in its best neighborhoods, and it also needs people to fill it. That's where immigrants can help. Cities like Dayton don't have direct control over immigration policy, but they can improve their chances of long-term success by being welcoming places for immigrants. This is not to say that immigration won't cause any problems for some people already in Dayton. While the research is somewhat mixed, there is evidence that particularly large influxes of immigrants in a short amount of time can push down wages for lower-skill native workers.[46] Other research in different contexts supports this idea, such as the Great Migration research we discussed

46. George J. Borjas, *"The Wage Impact of the Marielitos: Additional Evidence"* (Working Paper No. 21850, National Bureau of Economic Research, 2016).

earlier that found that southern blacks pushed down wages for northern blacks upon the former's arrival in northern cities.

That said, the large influxes of immigrants that put pressure on native workers' wages are rare. Most of the time, especially in cities away from the coasts such as Dayton, immigrants arrive at a reasonable rate that doesn't overwhelm the local labor market. And while they still compete with local workers for a variety of jobs, the slower pace of immigration gives employers and natives time to adjust.

It's also important to remember that people are resources. And if there is one resource a shrinking city needs more of, it's people. The labor of immigrants increases output in America, and more output means more consumption. Even if wages slightly decline or don't grow as fast for some lower-skill native workers, the additional output produced by immigrants helps keep prices low, and this tends to more than make up for the slightly lower wages. There's also evidence that high-skill immigrants raise wages for both college- and noncollege-educated native workers in cities.[47] It would be a mistake for city officials to associate all immigration with lower wages, since in many cases immigrants complement rather than crowd out native workers.

Immigrants also provide important variety that makes city living attractive. As we discussed earlier, downtowns in large cities are experiencing a comeback, and this comeback is driven by young college-educated workers who value a variety of consumption options. Immigrants are often the proprietors of unique stores, restaurants, bars, and other urban businesses that young, educated workers desire. By welcoming immigrants, Dayton increases the likelihood that its downtown becomes the center of variety in the Dayton metro area.

Often, supporters of immigration focus on the relatively few exceptional immigrants who start large companies that employ thousands of workers, native and immigrant alike. Examples include Sergey Brin (Russia) of Google, Elon Musk (South Africa) of Tesla and SpaceX, and Jerry Yang (Taiwan) of Yahoo. While these are great stories, they are the exception rather than the rule. Most immigrants, like most US natives, will not start Fortune 500 companies that can single-handedly revitalize a city like Dayton, and city officials are setting themselves up for disappointment if they use such stories to push for more immigration. But immigrants are typically hardworking people who positively impact an area's culture and economy in many smaller ways, and welcoming them should provide a net benefit to Dayton.

---

47. Giovanni Peri, Kevin Shih, and Chad Sparber, "STEM Workers, H-1B Visas, and Productivity in US Cities," *Journal of Labor Economics* 33, no. S1 (July 2015): S225–55.

Other Suggestions

Improved tax policy, a climate of permissionless innovation, and a more dynamic built environment will do more than just increase the number of jobs or raise wages in Dayton. They will improve the quality of life in the city. Unfortunately, misguided policy has exacerbated the labor market woes in many places. State regulations such as occupational licensing bear some of the blame. Occupational licensing rules require people to spend time and money completing government-mandated training before they can engage in certain occupations, such as barbers or heating, ventilation, and air conditioning (HVAC) contractors. Proponents of these rules claim they are necessary for safety reasons, but researchers have found little evidence that states without rules for certain occupations are less safe than states with rules.[48] Instead, occupational licensing tends to increase costs for consumers by limiting competition while providing little to no additional protection. And in places with a lot of unemployed former manufacturing workers, such as Dayton, occupational licensing makes it harder for those workers to transition to new jobs that are better suited for a modern service-sector economy. City officials don't directly control a lot of licensing, but they can and should encourage state lawmakers to reduce occupational licensing requirements when there are no legitimate safety issues.

Dayton should also resist the temptation to raise its minimum wage. Many cities have recently increased their minimum wage in an attempt to help lower-skill workers, but such increases often backfire and hurt the very workers city officials and voters say they want to help. For example, Seattle is in the process of increasing its minimum wage to $15 per hour, but recent research finds that the city's increase is actually reducing average monthly earnings since employers are responding by cutting back hours.[49] Other research finds that minimum wage increases reduce job growth, which hurts low-skill workers over time by eliminating job opportunities that otherwise would be available.[50] We have already seen that a large percentage of Dayton's less-educated working-age adults are not in the labor force, so

---

48. Morris M. Kleiner, "Reforming Occupational Licensing Policies," Brookings Institute Discussion Paper 2015–01 (2015).

49. Ekaterina Jardim et al., "*Minimum Wage Increases, Wages, and Low-Wage Employment: Evidence from Seattle*" (Working Paper No. 23532, National Bureau of Economic Research, 2017).

50. Jonathan Meer and Jeremy West, "Effects of the Minimum Wage on Employment Dynamics," *Journal of Human Resources* 51, no. 2 (2015): 500–22.

it doesn't make sense for city officials and voters to make it even harder for them to find a job by arbitrarily raising the minimum wage.

To attract and retain people, Dayton needs a competitive advantage. Its best strategy for creating one is to focus on the things it can control—taxes, regulation, and land-use restrictions. A policy of permissionless innovation will help the city become more dynamic, which should boost the economy and help the city adapt to future economic shocks. Welcoming immigrants is also important, since immigrants help create the variety of consumption options that young college-educated people want in their downtowns. The city should also reexamine its historic district rules, since those same young people and immigrants may not be attracted to 100-year-old houses. Some people might think these changes are too radical, but underdogs must often take radical steps to overtake the favorites, and right now Dayton is an underdog.

CHAPTER 7

Conclusion

In the old world, firms had to be in the city to exploit the
river and realize lower production and shipping costs
. . . In this new world, cities that are not cost effective or
that do not otherwise provide attractive environments
for high-quality workers and their firms decline.

—ECONOMIST JOSEPH GYOURKO[1]

DAYTON'S ECONOMIC decline was due to a variety of inter-
twined factors that are in some ways still working against it. For
example, the factors most out of its control, climate and geography, remain disadvantages. But luckily for Dayton, many cities with better climates and in better locations are doing everything they can to repel
people.

Since the late 1960s, cities around the San Francisco Bay, in Southern
California, and along the East Coast have adopted strict land-use regulations
that are driving up housing prices and limiting the amount of people who
live there. Common regulations include minimum lot sizes, minimum parking requirements, maximum building heights, and environmental reviews
that add length to construction time and increase uncertainty for develop-
ers. One study finds that in the typical community it takes about six months
from the time a building permit is requested to when a decision is made
about whether to approve it.[2] And as we discussed earlier, historic neighborhood designations also prevent certain types of construction and make it
difficult to add new housing.

---

1. Joseph Gyourko et al., "Looking Back to Look Forward," 1–58.
2. Joseph Gyourko, Albert Saiz, and Anita Summers. "A New Measure of the Local
Regulatory Environment for Housing Markets: The Wharton Residential Land Use Regulatory Index." *Urban Studies* 45, no. 3 (2008): 693–729.

Economist William Fischel attributes this phenomenon to what he calls the "homevoter" problem. Homeowners who are voters (hence "homevoters") have so much of their wealth tied up in their houses that they view any new building that may erode the value of their home as a threat to their financial security. As a result, they vote for policies that make building difficult, which keeps the supply of housing low. The result is artificially high housing prices in many cities on both coasts, which means more people are living inland in places like Dayton.

Three cities typically associated with strict land-use regulations that make it difficult to build new housing are San Francisco, San Jose, and New York. From 1990 to 2010, the populations of these cities increased by 11%, 21%, and 12%, respectively. Meanwhile, the populations of Houston and Dallas, where land-use regulations are typically weaker, grew by 29% and 31%. Of course, geography also plays a role in a city's ability to grow.[3] Inland cities like Houston and Dallas typically have more room to spread out than coastal cities like New York or San Francisco, which are bounded by water. But even when geography is accounted for, there is still strong evidence that land-use regulations limit construction and population density in cities like New York.[4]

These land-use regulations have a big impact on the distribution of people in America. If San Francisco, San Jose, and New York would have grown by around 30% between 1990 and 2010—like Dallas and Houston—those three cities combined would contain nearly 1.6 million more people, some of whom would have migrated from places like Dayton. In fact, economists have estimated that if New York, San Jose, and San Francisco reduced their land-use regulations to those of the typical city, the populations of those cities would increase substantially while the populations of midwestern cities like Youngstown, Ohio; Mansfield, Ohio; and Kokomo, Indiana would decline.[5] Another study comes to a similar conclusion. The authors estimate that if land-use regulations were returned to their 1980 levels nationwide,

3. Albert Saiz, "The Geographic Determinants of Housing Supply," *Quarterly Journal of Economics* 125, no. 3 (August 2010): 1253–96.

4. Joseph Gyourko and Albert Saiz, "Construction Costs and the Supply of Housing Structure," *Journal of Regional Science* 46, no. 4 (2006): 661–80; Edward L. Glaeser and Bryce A. Ward, "The Causes and Consequences of Land Use Regulation: Evidence from Greater Boston," *Journal of Urban Economics* 65, no. 3 (2009): 265–78.

5. Chang-Tai Hsieh and Enrico Moretti, "*Why Do Cities Matter? Local Growth and Aggregate Growth*" (Working Paper No. 21154, National Bureau of Economic Research, 2015).

California, New York, and the Mid-Atlantic region would expand by drawing in people from the South and Midwest.[6]

In other words, larger cities with better climates, stronger economies, and coastal amenities are currently giving cities like Dayton an opening. Some people who would otherwise leave cities like Dayton are sticking around because land-use regulations that limit the supply of housing in many of the most productive and amenity-filled cities make it too expensive to move. But this might not be the case forever. California's state assembly is trying to implement a law that would make it easier to build in California's cities.[7] In fact, state preemption of local zoning and land-use restrictions has become a popular topic among policy wonks. Its supporters believe that more state oversight or outright control of local zoning can solve the homevoter problem since state officials and voters are less likely to be concerned with protecting home values in certain cities than they are with encouraging statewide economic growth. That said, homevoters who want to protect their most valuable asset are powerful constituents in both local and state politics and are unlikely to surrender to state preemption without a struggle.

Cities should also be wary of state preemption going too far. The best way for Dayton to attract residents and businesses is by having a business climate that promotes innovation and entrepreneurship. But such a climate can only be created if Dayton can differentiate itself from other cities in Ohio and around the country. If Ohio creates policies that every local government must follow, there is no way for Dayton to separate itself from the pack. The same goes for federal policy. For example, if every city in Ohio levied the same taxes at the same rates, then tax policy would not be something that people or business would consider when making a location decision. As a result, other policies that cities could control, along with climate and geography, would determine where people lived.

Since geography and weather don't favor Dayton, especially in comparison to cities outside of Ohio, it's important for Dayton to retain some measure of local autonomy. This way, it can enact policies that compensate for its physical location and increase its attractiveness as a place to live and do business. Ohio's current home-rule law gives Dayton a fair amount of

6. Kyle F. Herkenhoff, Lee E. Ohanian, and Edward C. Prescott, "Tarnishing the Golden and Empire States: Land-Use Restrictions and the US Economic Slowdown," *Journal of Monetary Economics* 93 (January 2018): 89–109.

7. Roland Li, "Bill Could Add Millions of New Homes Next to California's Public Transit Stations," *San Francisco Business Times,* January 5, 2018, https://www.bizjournals.com/sanfrancisco/news/2018/01/05/scott-wiener-housing-bill-transit-development.html.

policy independence from the state, including control over tax rates, types of taxes levied, local business licensing, health and building codes, and land-use regulations, and Dayton's success hinges on its ability to use this control effectively. Otherwise, Dayton's inferior weather and geography, along with its recent history of decline, will determine its future.

Over the last 60 years, Dayton and many other midwestern cities have become economically stagnant. But it wasn't always like this. As we have seen, Dayton used to be one of the most innovative cities in the country. Successful cities are those that effectively leverage their most important feature—high population density. City policies that emphasize manufacturing or similar jobs are not leveraging the population density that gives cities their advantage. If Dayton is going to have a shot at future economic success, it needs to once again fulfill the economic roles of a city: specialization and innovation. This means city officials and voters need to be flexible in regard to regulation, fiscal policies such as taxes and government spending, and the city's built environment. Cities that try to hold on to a romanticized version of their past will be eclipsed by others that embrace change.

Dayton also needs to attract and retain talented people who care about the area. Home-grown businesses with ties to the community, not footloose companies attracted by tax breaks, are important for a city's success. And if home-grown companies leave, there needs to be a culture of innovation in place that doesn't hesitate to replace and replenish.

Chapter 6 provides some advice for Dayton officials and residents about how to improve the city's economy, but there is no silver bullet. That said, low taxes, a focus on core services to keep spending under control, a simple regulatory structure that minimizes uncertainty and compliance costs, a friendly environment for immigrants, and a policy of permissionless innovation that fosters a willingness to adapt can together create an environment that allows entrepreneurs to thrive in Dayton. Other cities in Dayton's position, such as Cleveland, Buffalo, Detroit, and Akron, would also benefit from these ideas.

Finally, city officials need to understand that they don't cause economic growth but that they can provide a foundation for growth. A competent government is important for long-term success, but so is an innovative private sector. As economist Ed Glaeser stated, "Private entrepreneurs, not public officials, power urban economies."[8]

---

8. Ed Glaeser, "A New Urban Opportunity Agenda," *City Journal*, Autumn 2015, http://www.city-journal.org/2015/25_4_urban-opportunity.html.

ACKNOWLEDGMENTS

Several people helped me make this book a reality. First, thanks to all my friends at the Mercatus Center at George Mason University who supported my initial study on Dayton, which I expanded into this book. In particular, Eileen Norcross, Emily Hamilton, and Bryce Chinault provided excellent comments on the study that I incorporated into this book. Garrett Brown was also an invaluable resource throughout the process of creating a book proposal and identifying a publisher. I also need to thank Kyle Precourt, who reads and edits much of my writing and in doing so makes me a better writer.

Next, thank you to my former colleagues at the L. Charles Hilton Jr. Center at Florida State University for your support, along with Sam Staley who read an early draft and provided helpful feedback. I learn a lot about economics from our conversations, which helped me write a better book.

Others have also helped me along the way through various bits of advice, economic insights, and friendship. Andy Swanson and Danielle Zanzalari are great sounding boards. My professors at Clemson University helped me hone the skills I needed to write this book. There are, of course, many others, and I want you all to know that I appreciate your support.

The people at The Ohio State University Press were also very helpful, especially Tony Sanfilippo, who pitched my book to the board and answered all my questions along the way. It was also great working with Laurie Avery, Tara Cyphers, Rebekah Cotton, and other OSU Press staff who contributed to the final product. I also want to thank two anonymous reviewers who provided constructive comments that improved the book. Any errors that remain are my own.

Finally, a big thank-you to my entire family. My father's family moved from Tennessee to the Dayton area in the mid-twentieth century as part of the migration event known as the Hillbilly Highway, and absent that serendipitous act I doubt I would have written this book. In fact, I was largely motivated to write this book to explain Dayton's experience to my family and, above all, I hope they like it. My wife Meredith and parents have been especially supportive of all my work, not just this book, and I am thankful to have them in my life.

BIBLIOGRAPHY

Adam A. Millsap. "How the Gem City Lost Its Luster and How It Can Get It Back." *SSRN Electronic Journal*, January 16, 2018. doi:10.2139/ssrn.3169568.

Adam A. Millsap. "Location Choice in Early Adulthood: Millennials versus Baby Boomers." *Papers in Regional Science* 97 (2018): S139–S167.

Adam A. Millsap. "The Role of Economic Freedom in Intercity Competition: A Framework and Some Evidence from US Metropolitan Areas." *Journal of Regional Analysis and Policy* 48, no. 2 (2018): 89–106.

Adam Smith. *An Inquiry Into the Nature and Causes of the Wealth of Nations*. London: T. Nelson and Sons, 1887.

Adam Thierer. *Permissionless Innovation: The Continuing Case for Comprehensive Technological Freedom*. Arlington, VA: Mercatus Center George Mason University, 2016.

Alan Peters and Peter Fisher. "The Failures of Economic Development Incentives." *Journal of the American Planning Association* 70, no. 1 (Winter 2004): 27–37.

Albert O. Hirschman. *Exit, Voice, and Loyalty: Responses to Decline in Firms, Organizations, and States*. Cambridge, MA: Harvard University Press, 1970.

Albert Saiz. "The Geographic Determinants of Housing Supply." *Quarterly Journal of Economics* 125, no. 3 (August 2010): 1253–96.

Alfred Marshall. *Principles of Economics: An Introductory Volume*. London: Macmillan, 1961.

Alfred Pritchard Sloan. *My Years with General Motors*. edited by John McDonald and Catharine Stevens. New York: Doubleday, 1963.

Alan DiGaetano. "Urban Political Reform:" Did It Kill the Machine?" *Journal of Urban History* 18, no. 1 (1991): 37–67.

Allan W. Eckert. *A Time of Terror: The Great Dayton Flood.* Santa Fe, NM: Landfall Press, 1965.

Andrea Caragliu, Chiara F. Del Bo, Karima Kourtit, and Peter Nijkamp. "The Winner Takes It All: Forward-Looking Cities and Urban Innovation." *Annals of Regional Science* 56, no. 3 (May 2016): 617–45.

Andrew Mair, Richard Florida, and Martin Kenney. "The New Geography of Automobile Production: Japanese Transplants in North America." *Economic Geography* 64, no. 4 (1988): 352–73.

Ann Bartel and David Lewin. "Wages and Unionism in the Public Sector: The Case of Police." *The Review of Economics and Statistics* 63, no. 1 (February 1981): 53–59.

Arthur E. Morgan. *The Miami Valley and the 1913 Flood: Technical Reports, Part 1.* Miami Conservancy District: Dayton, 1917.

Arthur Ernest Morgan. *The Miami Conservancy District.* New York: McGraw-Hill, 1951.

Ben S. Bernanke. "The Macroeconomics of the Great Depression: A Comparative Approach." *Journal of Money, Credit, and Banking* 27, no. 1 (1995): 1–28.

Benjamin Y. Clark. "Can Tax Expenditures Stimulate Growth in Rust Belt Cities?" In *The Road through the Rust Belt from Preeminence to Decline to Prosperity*, edited by William M. Bowen, 37–68. Kalamazoo, MI: Upjohn Institute for Employment Research, 2014.

C. Nardinelli and C. J. Simon. "Human Capital and the Rise of American Cities, 1900–1990." *Regional Science and Urban Economics* 32 (2002): 59–96.

C. Nardinelli and C. J. Simon. "The Talk of the Town: Human Capital, Information, and the Growth of English Cities, 1861 to 1961." *Explorations in Economic History* 33, no. 3 (1996) 384–413.

C. A. Bock. *History of the Miami Flood Control Project: Technical Reports, Part II.* Ann Arbor: University of Michigan Library, repr., 1918. 74.

Carl M. Campbell III and Kunal S. Kamlani. "The Reasons for Wage Rigidity: Evidence from a Survey of Firms." *Quarterly Journal of Economics* 112, no. 3 (1997): 759–89.

Carol MacLennan and J. O'Donnell. "The Effects of the Automotive Transition on Employment: A Plant and Community Study." Third Automotive Fuel Economy Research Contractor's Coordination Meeting, US DOT, NHTSA, December 1–2, 1980.

Chang-Tai Hsieh and Enrico Moretti, "Why Do Cities Matter? Local Growth and Aggregate Growth." *SSRN Electronic Journal*, 2015. doi:10.2139/ssrn.2693282.

Charles I. Jones. "R & D–based Models of Economic Growth." *Journal of Political Economy* 103, no. 4 (August 1995): 759–84.

Charles M. Tiebout. "A Pure Theory of Local Expenditures." *Journal of Political Economy* 64, no. 5 (October 1956): 416–24.

Chester Edward Rightor, Don Conger Sowers, and Walter Matscheck. *City Manager in Dayton: Four Years of Commission-Manager Government, 1914–1917; and Comparisons with Four Preceding Years Under the Mayor-Council Plan, 1910–1913.* New York: Macmillan, 1919.

Chris Edwards. "Public Sector Unions and the Rising Costs of Employee Compensation." *Cato Journal* 30 (2010): 87.

Christina D. Romer. "The Great Crash and the Onset of the Great Depression." *Quarterly Journal of Economics* 105, no. 3 (1990): 597–624.

Christopher J. Ruhm. "Deaths of Despair or Drug Problems?" The National Bureau of Economic Research, January 2018. doi:10.3386/w24188.

Cliff Ellis. "Interstate Highways, Regional Planning and the Reshaping of Metropolitan America." *Planning Practice and Research* 16, no. 3–4 (2001): 247–69.

Curtis Simon. "Human Capital and Metropolitan Employment Growth." *Journal of Urban Economics* 43, no. 2 (March 1998): 223–43.

Dagney Faulk. "Do State Economic Development Incentives Create Jobs? An Analysis of State Employment Tax Credits." *National Tax Journal* 55, no. 2 (June 2002): 263–80.

David Albouy and Bert Lue. "Driving to Opportunity: Local Rents, Wages, Commuting and Sub-Metropolitan Quality of Life." *Journal of Urban Economics* 89 (September 2015): 74–92.

David L. Birch. *Job Creation in Cities.* Cambridge, MA: MIT Program on Neighborhood and Regional Change, 1980.

David McCullough. *The Wright Brothers.* New York: Simon and Schuster, 2015.

David Neumark, Brandon Wall, and Junfu Zhang. "Do Small Businesses Create More Jobs? New Evidence for the United States from the National Establishment Time Series." *Review of Economics and Statistics* 93, no. 1 (February 2011): 16–29.

David R. Meyer. "The Industrial Retardation of Southern Cities, 1860–1880." *Explorations in Economic History* 25, no. 4 (1988): 366–86.

David W. Jones Jr. *Urban Transit Policy: An Economic and Political History.* Englewood Cliffs, NJ: Prentice Hall, 1985.

Dean B. Stansel. "An Economic Freedom Index for US Metropolitan Areas." *Journal of Regional Analysis and Policy* 43, no. 1 (2013): 3–20.

Dennis Coates. "Growth Effects of Sports Franchises, Stadiums, and Arenas: 15 Years Later." *SSRN Electronic Journal,* September 2018. doi:10.2139/ssrn.3191302.

Dionissi Aliprantis and Anne Chen. "The Opioid Epidemic and the Labor Market." *Economic Commentary, Federal Reserve Bank of Cleveland.* September 29, 2017.

Douglas Nelson. "The Political Economy of US Automobile Protection." In *The Political Economy of American Trade Policy,* edited by Anne O. Krueger, 133–96. University of Chicago Press, 1996.

Douglas S. Massey and Nancy A. Denton. "Suburbanization and Segregation in US Metropolitan Areas." *American Journal of Sociology* 94, no. 3 (November 1988): 592–626.

Duncan Black and Vernon Henderson. "A Theory of Urban Growth." *Journal of Political Economy* 107, no. 2 (1999): 252–84.

Edward J. Malecki. "Dimensions of R & D Location in the United States." *Research Policy* 9, no. 1 (1980): 2–22.

Edward L. Glaeser. "Cities, Information, and Economic Growth." *Cityscape* 1, no. 1 (1994): 9–47.

Edward L. Glaeser. "Reinventing Boston: 1630–2003." *Journal of Economic Geography* 5, no. 2 (2005): 119–53.

Edward L. Glaeser and Albert Saiz. "The Rise of the Skilled City." The National Bureau of Economic Research, 2003. doi:10.3386/w10191.

Edward L. Glaeser and Bryce A. Ward. "The Causes and Consequences of Land Use Regulation: Evidence from Greater Boston." *Journal of Urban Economics* 65, no. 3 (2009): 265–78.

Edward L. Glaeser, Giacomo A. M. Ponzetto, and Kristina Tobio. "Cities, Skills and Regional Change." *Regional Studies* 48, no. 1 (2014): 7–43.

Edward L. Glaeser, Hedi D. Kallal, José A. Scheinkman, and Andrei Shleifer. "Growth in Cities." *Journal of Political Economy* 100, no. 6 (1992): 1126–52.

Edward L. Glaeser, Jed Kolko, and Albert Saiz. "Consumer City." *Journal of Economic Geography* 1, no. 1 (2001): 27–50.

Edward L. Glaeser and Jesse M. Shapiro. "Urban Growth in the 1990s: Is City Living Back?" *Journal of Regional Science* 43, no. 1 (2003): 139–65.

Edward L. Glaeser and Matthew E. Kahn. "Decentralized Employment and the Transformation of the American City." *Brookings-Wharton Papers on Urban Affairs* 2001, no. 1 (2001): 1–63.

Ekaterina Jardim, Mark C. Long, Robert Plotnick, Emma van Inwegen, Jacob Vigdor, and Hilary Wething. "Minimum Wage Increases, Wages, and Low-Wage Employment: Evidence from Seattle." The National Bureau of Economic Research, May 2017. doi:10.3386/w23532.

Emily C. Skarbek. "The Chicago Fire of 1871: A Bottom-Up Approach to Disaster Relief." *Public Choice* 160, no. 1–2 (July 2014): 155–80.

Enrico Moretti. "Local Multipliers." *American Economic Review* 100, no. 2 (2010): 373–77.

Eric Joseph van Holm. "Minor Stadiums, Major Effects? Patterns and Sources of Redevelopment Surrounding Minor League Baseball Stadiums." *Urban Studies* 56, no. 4 (2018): 672–88. doi:10.1177/0042098018760731.

Finis Welch. "Black-White Differences in Returns to Schooling." *American Economic Review* 63, no. 5 (December 1973): 893–907.

Ford, Frank, April Hirsh, Kathryn Clover, Jeffrey A. Marks, Robin Dubin, Michael Schramm, Tsui Chan, Nina Lalich, Andrew Loucky, and Natalia Cabrera. "The Role of Investors in The One-To-Three Family REO Market: The Case of Cleveland." Joint Center for Housing Studies, Harvard University, December 16, 2013. https://www.jchs.harvard.edu/sites/default/files/w13-12_cleveland_0.pdf.

G. D. Padfield and B. Lawrence. "The Birth of Flight Control: An Engineering Analysis of the Wright Brothers' 1902 Glider." *Aeronautical Journal* 107, no. 1078 (December 2003): 697–718.

George J. Borjas. "The Wage Impact of the Marielitos: Additional Evidence." The National Bureau of Economic Research, 2016. doi:10.3386/w21850.

Georgeanne M. Artz, Kevin Duncan, Arthur P. Hall, and Peter F. Orazem. "Do State Business Climate Indicators Explain Relative Economic Growth at State Borders?" *Journal of Regional Science* 56, no. 3 (2016): 395–419.

Giovanni Peri, Kevin Shih, and Chad Sparber. "STEM Workers, H-1B Visas, and Productivity in US Cities." *Journal of Labor Economics* 33, no. S1 (July 2015): S225–55.

Gregory M. Saltzman. "Public Sector Bargaining Laws Really Matter: Evidence from Ohio and Illinois." In *When Public Sector Workers Unionize*, edited by Richard B. Freeman and Casey Ichniowski, 41–80. Chicago, IL: University of Chicago Press, 1988.

Harold L. Cole and Lee E. Ohanian. "The Great Depression in the United States from a Neoclassical Perspective." *Handbook of Monetary and Fiscal Policy* 1 (2001): 159.

Heike Delfmann and Sierdjan Koster. "The Effect of New Business Creation on Employment Growth in Regions Facing Population Decline." *Annals of Regional Science* 56, no. 1 (2016): 33–54.

Herbert A. Johnson. "The Wright Patent Wars and Early American Aviation." *Journal of Air Law and Commerce* 69, no. 1 (2004): 21.

Ingrid Gould Ellen and Katherine O'Regan. "Crime and Urban Flight Revisited: The Effect of the 1990s Drop in Crime on Cities." *Journal of Urban Economics* 68, no. 3 (2010): 247–59.

Irwin Feller. "The Urban Location of United States Invention, 1860–1910." *Explorations in Economic History* 8, no. 3 (1971): 285–303.

Isaac Frederick Marcosson. *Colonel Deeds: Industrial Builder.* New York: Dodd, Mead, 1947.

J. Fred Giertz. "An Experiment in Public Choice: The Miami Conservancy District, 1913–1922." *Public Choice* 19, no. 1 (1974): 63–75.

J. Stephen Ferris and Edwin G. West. "The Cost Disease and Government Growth: Qualifications to Baumol." *Public Choice* 89, no. 1–2 (1996): 35–52.

James B. Bailey and Diana W. Thomas. "Regulating Away Competition: The Effect of Regulation on Entrepreneurship and Employment." *Journal of Regulatory Economics* 52, no. 3 (December 2017): 237–54.

James E. Rauch. "Bureaucracy, Infrastructure, and Economic Growth: Evidence from US Cities during the Progressive Era." *American Economic Review* 85, no. 4 (February 1995): 968–79.

James M. Rubenstein. "Changing Distribution of the American Automobile Industry." *Geographical Review* 76, no. 3 (July 1986): 288–300.

James Weinstein. "Organized Business and the City Commission and Manager Movements." *Journal of Southern History* 28, no. 2 (May 1962): 166–82.

Jamie Bologna, Andrew T. Young, and Donald J. Lacombe. "A Spatial Analysis of Incomes and Institutional Quality: Evidence from US Metropolitan Areas." *Journal of Institutional Economics* 12, no. 1 (March 2016): 191–216.

Jan K. Brueckner. *Lectures on Urban Economics.* Cambridge, MA: MIT Press, 2011.

Jan K. Brueckner and Stuart S. Rosenthal. "Gentrification and Neighborhood Housing Cycles: Will America's Future Downtowns Be Rich?" *Review of Economics and Statistics* 91, no. 4 (November 2009): 725–43.

Jane Jacobs. *The Economy of Cities.* New York: Vintage, 1970.

Jason Barr and Troy Tassier. "The Dynamics of Subcenter Formation: Midtown Manhattan, 1861–1906." *Journal of Regional Science* 56, no. 5 (2016): 754–91.

Jed Kolko, David Neumark, and Marisol Cuellar Mejia. "What Do Business Climate Indexes Teach Us about State Policy and Economic Growth?" *Journal of Regional Science* 53, no. 2 (2013): 220–55.

Jeffrey Zax and Casey Ichniowski. "The Effects of Public Sector Unionism on Pay, Employment, Department Budgets, and Municipal Expenditures." In *When Public Sector Workers Unionize,* edited by Richard B. Freeman and Casey Ichniowski, 323–64. Chicago, IL: University of Chicago Press, 1988.

Jesse J. Richardson, Meghan Zimmerman Gough, and Robert Puentes. "Is Home Rule the Answer?: Clarifying the Influence of Dillon's Rule on Growth Management." Center on Urban and Metropolitan Policy, the Brookings Institution, January 1 2003.

John Dove. "Local Government Type and Municipal Bond Ratings: What's the Relationship?" *Applied Economics* 49, no. 24 (2017): 2339–51.

John R. Schleppi. "'It Pays': John H. Patterson and Industrial Recreation at the National Cash Register Company." *Journal of Sport History* 6, no. 3 (1979): 20–28.

John Siegfried and Andrew Zimbalist. "The Economics of Sports Facilities and Their Communities." *Journal of Economic Perspectives* 14, no. 3 (Summer 2000): 95–114.

Jon M. Hawes and John H. Patterson. "Leaders in Selling and Sales Management: John H. Patterson." *Journal of Personal Selling & Sales Management* 5, no. 2 (1985): 59–61.

Jonathan Meer and Jeremy West. "Effects of the Minimum Wage on Employment Dynamics." *Journal of Human Resources* 51, no. 2 (2015): 500–22.

Jordan Rappaport. "Moving to Nice Weather." *Regional Science and Urban Economics* 37, no. 3 (2007): 375–98.

Joseph A. Schumpeter. *Capitalism, Socialism and Democracy.* London: Routledge, 2013.

Joseph Gyourko and Albert Saiz. "Construction Costs and the Supply of Housing Structure." *Journal of Regional Science* 46, no. 4 (2006): 661–80.

Joseph Gyourko, Albert Saiz, and Anita Summers. "A New Measure of the Local Regulatory Environment for Housing Markets: The Wharton Residential Land Use Regulatory Index." *Urban Studies* 45, no. 3 (2008): 693–729.

Joseph Gyourko, Robert A. Margo, and Andrew F. Haughwout. "Looking Back to Look Forward: Learning from Philadelphia's 350 Years of Urban Development [with Comments]." *Brookings-Wharton Papers on Urban Affairs* (2005): 1–58.

Joseph Watras. "The Racial Desegregation of Dayton, Ohio, Public Schools, 1966–2008." *Ohio History* 117, no. 1 (2010): 93–107.

Josiah Grover, Erin Meyer, Jose Pacas, and Matthew Sobek. IPUMS USA: Version 8.0 [dataset]. Minneapolis, MN: IPUMS, 2018.

Judith Sealander. *Great Plans: Business Progressivism and Social Change in Ohio's Miami Valley 1890–1929.* Lexington: University of Kentucky Press, 1988.

Julie Berry Cullen and Steven D. Levitt. "Crime, Urban Flight, and the Consequences for Cities." *Review of Economics and Statistics* 81, no. 2 (May 1999): 159–69.

Kathy Hayes and Semoon Chang. "The Relative Efficiency of City Manager and Mayor-Council Forms of Government." *Southern Economic Journal* 57, no. 1 (July 1990): 167–77.

Keith Ihlanfeldt and Tom Mayock. "Foreclosures and Local Government Budgets." *Regional Science and Urban Economics* 53 (2015): 135–47.

Kevin M. O'Brien. "Compensation, Employment, and the Political Activity of Public Employee Unions." *Journal of Labor Research* 13 no. 2 (1992): 189–203.

Kevin T. Deno and Stephen L. Mehay. "Municipal Management Structure and Fiscal Performance: Do City Managers Make a Difference?" *Southern Economic Journal* 53, no. 3 (January 1987): 627–42.

Kyle F. Herkenhoff, Lee E. Ohanian, and Edward C. Prescott. "Tarnishing the Golden and Empire States: Land-Use Restrictions and the US Economic Slowdown." *Journal of Monetary Economics* 93 (January 2018): 89–109.

Leah P. Boustan. "Was Postwar Suburbanization 'White Flight'? Evidence from the Black Migration." *Quarterly Journal of Economics* 125, no. 1 (2010): 417–43.

Leah Platt Boustan. *Competition in the Promised Land: Black Migrants in Northern Cities and Labor Markets.* Princeton, NJ: Princeton University Press, 2016.

Leah Platt Boustan. "Local Public Goods and the Demand for High-Income Municipalities." *Journal of Urban Economics* 76 (2013): 71–82.

Leah Platt Boustan. "School Desegregation and Urban Change: Evidence from City Boundaries." *American Economic Journal: Applied Economics* 4, no. 1 (2012): 85–108.

Lee Iacocca. *Iacocca: An Autobiography.* New York: Bantam Books, 1984.

Liang Zheng. "What City Amenities Matter in Attracting Smart People?" *Papers in Regional Science* 95 (June 2016): 309–27.

Loren Gatch. "Tax Anticipation Scrip as a Form of Local Currency in the USA during the 1930s." *International Journal of Community Currency Research* 16 (2012): D22–35.

Marius Brülhart, Sam Bucovetsky, and Kurt Schmidheiny. "Taxes in Cities." *Handbook of Regional and Urban Economics* 5 (2015): 1123–96.

Martin Andersson and Johan P. Larsson. "Local Entrepreneurship Clusters in Cities." *Journal of Economic Geography* 16, no. 1 (January 2016): 39–66.

Metropolitan Community Studies. *Metropolitan Challenge: Study of the People, the Government, and the Economy of Metropolitan Dayton.* Dayton, Ohio, 1959.

Michael D. LaFaive and Michael J. Hicks. *"MEGA: A Retrospective Assessment."* Mackinac Center for Public Policy, 2005.

Michael E. Porter. "New Strategies for Inner-City Economic Development." *Economic Development Quarterly* 11, no. 1 (1998): 11–27.

Michael Storper. "Why Do Regions Develop and Change? The Challenge for Geography and Economics." *Journal of Economic Geography* 11, no. 2 (2010): 333–46. doi:10.1093/jeg/lbq033.

Morris M. Kleiner. "Reforming Occupational Licensing Policies." Brookings Institute Discussion Paper 2015–1, 2015.

Nathaniel Baum-Snow. "Did Highways Cause Suburbanization?" *Quarterly Journal of Economics* 122, no. 2 (May 2007): 775–805.

Orville Wright. "How We Made the First Flight." Department of Transportation, Federal Aviation Administration, Office of General Aviation Affairs, 1977.

Paul M. Romer. "Endogenous Technological Change." *The Journal of Political Economy* 98, no. 5 (October 1990): S71–102. doi:10.3386/w3210.

Philip N. Johnson-Laird. "Flying Bicycles: How the Wright Brothers Invented the Airplane." *Mind & Society* 4, no. 1 (2005): 27–48.

Price V. Fishback. "How Successful Was the New Deal? The Microeconomic Impact of New Deal Spending and Lending Policies in the 1930s." The National Bureau of Economic Research, 2016. doi:10.3386/w21925.

Randall G. Holcombe and DeEdgra W. Williams. "The Impact of Population Density on Municipal Government Expenditures." *Public Finance Review* 36, no. 3 (2008): 359–73.

Richard E. Wagner. *Deficits, Debt, and Democracy: Wrestling with Tragedy on the Fiscal Commons.* Northampton, MA: Edward Elgar Publishing, 2012.

Richard K. Green and Susan M. Wachter. "The American Mortgage in Historical and International Context." *Journal of Economic Perspectives* 19, no. 4 (Fall 2005): 93–114.

Robert A. Baade and Richard F. Dye. "The Impact of Stadium and Professional Sports on Metropolitan Area Development." *Growth and Change* 21, no. 2 (1990): 1–14.

Robert A. Margo. "Employment and Unemployment in the 1930s." *Journal of Economic Perspectives* 7, no. 2 (1993): 41–59.

Robert Bruegmann. *Sprawl: A Compact History.* Chicago: University of Chicago Press, 2005.

Rosenthal and Strange. "The Attenuation of Human Capital Spillovers." *Journal of Urban Economics* 64, no. 2 (September 2008): 373–89

Samuel Crowther. *John H. Patterson: Pioneer in Industrial Welfare.* New York: Garden City Publishing Co., 1926.

Samuel Staley. *Enterprise Zones and Inner City Economic Development: An Analysis of Firms in the Dayton, Ohio Enterprise Zone Program.* Dayton, OH: Center for Urban and Public Affairs, Wright State University, 1989.

Shahid Yusuf. "Intermediating Knowledge Exchange between Universities and Businesses." *Research Policy* 37, no. 8 (September 2008): 1173.

Shawn Kantor and Alexander Whalley. "Knowledge Spillovers from Research Universities: Evidence from Endowment Value Shocks." *Review of Economics and Statistics* 96, no. 1 (2014): 171–88.

Simeon Alder, David Lagakos, and Lee Ohanian. "Labor Market Conflict and the Decline of the Rust Belt." Manuscript, University of California, San Diego, 2017.

Stuart S. Rosenthal and William C. Strange. "Geography, Industrial Organization, and Agglomeration." *Review of Economics and Statistics* 85, no. 2 (2003): 377–93.

T. A. Boyd. "The Charles F. Kettering Archives." *Technology and Culture* 5, no. 3 (1964): 412–15.

Terry F. Buss. "The Effect of State Tax Incentives on Economic Growth and Firm Location Decisions: An Overview of the Literature." *Economic Development Quarterly* 15, no. 1 (February 2001): 90–105.

Thomas C. Schelling. "Models of Segregation." *American Economic Review* 59, no. 2 (1969): 488–93.

Thomas Flygare. "Dayton II: School Desegregation on a Roller Coaster." *Phi Delta Kappan* 61, no. 2 (1979): 124–25.

Todd M. Gabe and David S. Kraybill. "The Effect of State Economic Development Incentives on Employment Growth of Establishments." *Journal of Regional Science* 42, no. 4 (2002): 703–30.

Todd C. Neumann, Price V. Fishback, and Shawn Kantor. "The Dynamics of Relief Spending and the Private Urban Labor Market during the New Deal." *Journal of Economic History* 70, no. 1 (2010): 195–220.

Tom Hanchett. "The Other 'Subsidized Housing': Federal Aid to Suburbanization, 1940s–1960s." In *From Tenements to Taylor Homes: In Search of Urban Housing Policy in*

Twentieth Century America, edited by Roger Biles and Kristin Szylvian, 163–79. University Park, PA: Pennsylvania State University Press, 2000.

Victor Couture and Jessie Handbury. "Urban Revival in America, 2000 to 2010." The National Bureau of Economic Research, 2017. doi:10.3386/w24084.

Walter A. Friedman. "John H. Patterson and the Sales Strategy of the National Cash Register Company, 1884 to 1922." *Business History Review* 72, no. 4 (1998): 552–84.

Walter C. Rucker and James N. Upton, eds. *Encyclopedia of American Race Riots.* Vol. 2. Westport, CT: Greenwood Publishing Group, 2007.

Wayne Winegarden. "The 50-State Small Business Regulation Index." Pacific Research Institute, July 2015.

William F. Fox and Matthew N. Murray. "Do Economic Effects Justify the Use of Fiscal Incentives?" *Southern Economic Journal* 71, no. 1 (July 2004): 78–92.

William H. Frey."Central City White Flight: Racial and Nonracial Causes." *American Sociological Review* 44, no. 3 (June 1979): 425–48.

William J. Baumol. "Macroeconomics of Unbalanced Growth: The Anatomy of Urban Crisis." *The American Economic Review* 57, no. 3 (June 1967): 415–26.

William J. Carrington, Enrica Detragiache, and Tara Vishwanath. "Migration with Endogenous Moving Costs." *American Economic Review* 86, no. 4 (September 1996): 909–30.

William J. Collins. "When the Tide Turned: Immigration and the Delay of the Great Black Migration." *Journal of Economic History* 57, no. 3 (1997): 607–32.

Yong Chen and Stuart S. Rosenthal. "Local Amenities and Life-Cycle Migration: Do People Move for Jobs or Fun?" *Journal of Urban Economics* 64, no. 3 (November 2008): 519–37.

ABOUT THE AUTHOR

Adam A. Millsap is Senior Fellow, Economic Opportunity at the Charles Koch Institute.

He conducts research on urban development, population trends, labor markets, and federal, state, and local public policy. His op-eds and commentary have appeared in national outlets such as *Forbes, USA Today,* Real Clear Policy, and *US News and World Report,* as well as regional outlets such as the *Detroit Free Press, Orlando Sentinel, Cincinnati Enquirer,* and *Orange County Register,* among others.

In addition to his research and writing, he has taught courses in economics at the undergraduate and graduate level at Florida State University, Clemson University, and George Mason University.

He earned his master's and PhD in economics from Clemson University and a BS in economics and a BA in comparative religion from Miami University.